# LENGTHEN

## YOUR

# SHUFFLE

# LENGTHEN

## YOUR

# SHUFFLE

A GUIDEBOOK FOR SENIOR MISSIONARIES

## ED J. PINEGAR

Covenant Communications, Inc.

Cover photography "Picture This . . . by Sara Staker"

Cover design copyrighted 2002 by Covenant Communications, Inc.

Published by Covenant Communications, Inc.
American Fork, Utah

Printed in the United States of America
First Printing: February 2002

09 08 07 06 05 04 03 02    10 9 8 7 6 5 4 3 2 1

ISBN 1-57734-980-6

**Library of Congress Cataloging-in-Publication Data**

Pinegar, Ed J.
    Lengthen your shuffle: a guidebook for senior missionaries/ Ed J. Pinegar.
        p.    cm.
    Includes biographical references.
    ISBN 1-57734-980-6 (alk. paper)
    1. Mormon missionaries--Religious life. I. Title

    BX8661.P565 2002
    266'.9332--dc21
                            20021058393

*Dedication*
*To all the magnificent senior missionaries who give so freely to build up the kingdom of God. And especially to those who I have had the honor of serving with.*

# ACKNOWLEDGEMENTS

Great thanks go to Shauna Nelson, Angela Colvin, and Katie Child for their wonderful support and excellent editorial skills, and to Maren Ogden for designing such a marvelous cover. I also appreciate Nola Delange for her efforts in typing the manuscript. And finally, I want to acknowledge all the senior missionaries who have taught me so much in the missionary effort.

# TABLE OF CONTENTS

Note: All italics throughout the book are the author's added emphasis unless otherwise noted in the citation.

# CHAPTER 1

## BUILDING UP THE KINGDOM OF GOD:

## WHY YOU ARE NEEDED

We often talk about the threefold mission of the Church. In this dispensation—especially in *this* dispensation—we have been commanded to proclaim the gospel, to perfect the Saints, and to redeem the dead. Why is this so important? Because everything that the Church, which is the kingdom of God upon the earth, does is for one purpose, and that is to assist in Heavenly Father's work: bringing to pass "the immortality and eternal life of man" (Moses 1:39).

In other words, Heavenly Father's priority is His children. Now I don't know what that does for you, but that gives me eternal self-esteem because I, Ed Jolley Pinegar, am Heavenly Father's son, and you are His sons and daughters. And the greatest thing you'll ever do on this earth is to help one of His children return home.

This concept is beautifully illustrated by the Prophet Joseph Smith's retranslation of Matthew 6:33, "Seek ye first the kingdom of God, and his righteousness; and all these things shall be added unto you." In the Joseph Smith translation of the Bible that verse now reads, "Seek ye first to *build up* the kingdom of God, *and to establish* his righteousness; and all these things shall be added unto you" (JST—Matt 6:38). Build up the kingdom! What is the kingdom made of? Men and women. You and me. When you bless someone's life, you elevate your own life. When you've "done it unto one of the least of these my brethren," the Savior said, you've "done it unto me" (Matt. 25:40). We must catch the vision of the worth of souls. Once you understand the worth of a soul, you'll want to share the gospel of

Jesus Christ. You'll want to help other people be happy because it's the only way you'll ever be happy on this earth and in the hereafter.

To learn that principle is why the Lord gave us families. Sister Pinegar and I were blessed with a large family, and I want you to know that all eight of them came on this earth as investigators. We taught all eight of them, and all eight were baptized. Therefore we have eight converts in our family. You can imagine how much Sister Pinegar and I grew trying to convert eight magnificent investigators! And now our kids are grown up. But unfortunately, as the Lord's children, Sister Pinegar and I aren't grown up yet. The Lord doesn't want us to simply stop growing because our own kids are out of the house. If you don't seek to serve, and seek to bless, it's very difficult to grow.

And it's continual growth that increases our capacity for joy. Why do you think all the missionaries come home and say the same thing at the pulpit? "It was the happiest eighteen months of my life! It was the greatest two years of my life!" Because great missionaries have attained the vision: the desire to continually build up the kingdom of God. And that vision is the key to growing and finding joy.

One time I was talking with an elderly gentlemen of about eighty years old. He related this conversation he'd had with Elder Haight. He said, "Well, Elder Haight, I'm so old I might die on my mission."

Elder Haight answered, "What a great place to die!"

Think about it. There could be no better thing to do or place to be than serving your God and your fellowmen. This earth was made only to provide an opportunity to test ourselves, to prove ourselves worthy. We need the vision of saving souls; and that's why you, the noble and great, were preserved to come forth at this time, to do all these wonderful things.

What a blessing to be preserved for the last days, to see the glorious culmination of God's work on earth. And with that blessing we have a responsibility. Regarding that duty, the Lord revealed section 138 of the Doctrine and Covenants to the prophet Joseph F. Smith:

> I observed that they were also among the noble and great ones who were chosen in the beginning to be rulers in the Church of God. Even before they were born, they with many

others, received their first lessons in the world of spirits and were prepared to come forth in the due time of the Lord to labor in his vineyard for the salvation of the souls of men (D&C 138:55–56).

## The Worth of a Soul

The Lord made it clear: "Remember the worth of souls is great in the sight of God; For, behold, the Lord your Redeemer suffered death in the flesh; wherefore he suffered the pain of all men, that all men might repent and come unto him. . . . And how great is his joy in the soul that repenteth!" (D&C 18:10–13). The Lord wants His children back, and the last days are here. Never has there been a time when the Lord has needed more disciples to do His work. This is the last time the vineyard will be pruned.

> And it came to pass that the Lord of the vineyard sent his servant; and the servant went and did as the Lord had commanded him, and brought other servants; and *they were few* [In other words, we are all that the Lord has].
>
> And the Lord of the vineyard said unto them: Go to, and labor in the vineyard, with your might. For behold, this is the last time that I shall nourish my vineyard; for the end is nigh at hand, and the season speedily cometh; and if ye labor with your might with me ye shall have joy in the fruit which I shall lay up unto myself against the time which will soon come.
>
> And it came to pass that the servants did go and labor with their mights; and the Lord of the vineyard labored also with them; and they did obey the commandments of the Lord of the vineyard in all things.
>
> And there began to be the natural fruit again in the vineyard; and the natural branches began to grow and thrive exceedingly; and the wild branches began to be plucked off and to be cast away; and they did keep the root and the top thereof equal, according to the strength thereof (Jacob 5:70–73).

This is our role. Now is the time. We are the ones to go into the vineyard to bring souls unto Christ. This is not a battle that should be left just to the young. We are not to waste out our remaining days in rocking chairs! I love the prophet Gordon B. Hinckley's words:

> I am no longer a young man filled with energy and vitality. . . . I'm given to meditation and prayer. I would enjoy sitting in a rocker, swallowing prescriptions, listening to soft music, and contemplating the things of the universe. But such activity offers no challenge and makes no contribution.
>
> I wish to be up and doing. I wish to face each day with resolution and purpose. I wish to use every waking hour to give encouragement, to bless those whose burdens are heavy, to build faith and strength of testimony. . . . It is the presence of wonderful people which stimulates the adrenaline. It is the look of love in their eyes which gives me energy ("Testimony," *Ensign,* May 1998, 69).

As President Hinkley says, the work we are all called to do is a work of love—that is the kind of work that makes life worth living. It is the whole basis of the Father's plan: "For God so *loved* the world, that he gave his only begotten Son" (John 3:16). Why did God give his only begotten Son? Because nothing is so precious as the souls of Heavenly Father's children. The whole work of Heavenly Father and our Savior is our immortality and eternal life (see Moses 1:39). Everything they do is for us—premortal life, the creation, a savior after the Fall, the plan of happiness, His gospel, the kingdom of God, and the resurrection of all mankind. Christ came that He might provide a way for all mankind to return, especially the lost sheep (see Matt. 18:11), for His joy is in our salvation.

There is great joy—both in the heavens and in mortality—over those who repent (see Luke 15:10; D&C 18:13). The sons of Mosiah could not bear the thought of some of their brothers and sisters perishing, and that included the Lamanites—their enemies! (see Mosiah 28:3). Alma also described his feelings for the souls of men as he taught his son Corianton: "And now I will ease your mind somewhat on this subject. Behold, you marvel why these things should be known so long beforehand. Behold, I say unto you, is not a soul at this time as precious unto God as a soul will be at the time of his coming?" (Alma 39:17).

The Whitmer brothers, Peter and John, were taught what was of most worth. Was it a new car, a new home, a motor home, clothes, money, vacations, time off, cruises, honor, or fortune? No, they were told, "And now, behold, I say unto you, that the thing which will be of the most worth unto you will be to declare repentance unto this people, that you may bring souls unto me, that you may rest with them in the kingdom of my Father" (D&C 15:6).

Christ's beloved disciple, John, also caught the vision of the worth of souls. Elder Holland described the event:

> The Apostle John asked the Lord if he, John, might remain on the earth beyond the normal span of life for no other purpose than to bring more souls unto God. In granting that wish, the Savior said that this was "a greater work" and a "nobler desire" even than that of desiring to come into the presence of the Lord "speedily."
>
> Like all prophets and apostles, the Prophet Joseph Smith understood the deep meaning of John's request when he said, "After all that has been said, [our] greatest and most important duty is to preach the Gospel" (Jeffery R. Holland, "Witness unto Me," *Ensign*, May 2001, 16).

### Joy in Service

Hand in hand with the duty to preach the gospel are the exalting blessings of joy—and all the other amazing feelings the Lord gives us by the Spirit to strengthen us. Elder LeGrand Richards described his thoughts on this phenomenon: "I have said to my wife time and time again, 'Of all the things that God has created . . . the most marvelous thing that he has created is the feelings of the human breast'" (*The Things That Matter*, BYU Speeches of the Year [1961], 1–9).

I have witnessed this "most marvelous thing" with young and senior missionaries alike as they have called or written their new friends—whether a new convert or newly reactivated member of the

Church. Their joy is indescribable. Their gratitude to God is beyond expression. Their newfound friendships are centered in Christ and the joy of the gospel. Here are some of the feelings senior missionaries have expressed:

> This is our second mission. Our first one [was] to the North Carolina Charlotte Mission, 1999, to a small branch in Sparte, N. C. (top of the Blue Ridge Mountains). All but two of the branch membership are converts. There were fifty-one members at the time, with seventeen attending. We were sent there to serve by our Lord and Savior. Through us, He activated most of the members and they gave up [the] contention that caused their inactivity. Today the branch has grown and is healthy and will soon get a new (their first) chapel in Allegheny County.
>
> I can't express the joy we had in serving that mission. Five new converts, "new move-ins," temple endowments, and a new convert sealing in the Raleigh Temple. They are our family. We love them to pieces. We are just as excited to go to the Mormon Handcart Visitors' Center. We expect that if we are faithful and humble our Savior will use us again to bless His children who come there. These missions for seniors are the best.
>
> All it takes to do this is love, visit, love, visit, visit and love and learn how to "flatfoot" dance with them.
>
> —Elder and Sister Clement

And the joy of missionary work is a two-way street. For example, I remember when a young girl came up to me and said, "Oh, President Pinegar, I'm so happy. The senior missionary couple in our ward is so wonderful. They saved me and my family. I can never thank them enough. I owe my life to them." Here is another example of the same kind of miracle. Elder and Sister Fraser tell of their experiences changing the world and the lives of God's children:

We were leadership missionaries in the Guatemala City South Mission in 1995–96. Elder Fraser was called to be the branch president in the Taxisco branch and the district president of the district of Guazacapas in the department of Santa Rosa. Even though our Spanish was limited, we were able to communicate with the people whom we loved dearly.

We could read and write, which many of the members could not. We had one 73-year-old sister who was so faithful and strong and an example for all. There had been many problems in the branch and it was closed for some time. During that time, she never wavered or left the church as many members did. She remained strong, and [she] was so happy when we arrived and opened the branch again.

She shared her testimony so many times about the truthfulness of the Book of Mormon, even though she had never read it because she couldn't read or write. When the missionaries taught her, they would read to her from the Book of Mormon, and she felt the Spirit and knew that it was true. She is raising grandchildren and great-grandchildren and each night they read the Book of Mormon. Even though we have been home for five years, we still receive letters from her (written by others) and she assures us that she is still firm in the gospel.

—Elder Duane and Sister Shirley Fraser

This story has been repeated in many different ways, but with the same message. The senior missionaries made all the difference in blessing the nonmembers, the part-member families, and the less active. They have made—and can make—the difference in the lives of hundreds of thousands of members of the Church.

In a desire for the Saints to feel the joy of this work, the prophet Heber J. Grant recorded:

I want you young [and not-so-young] people to know that [of] all my labors I got nearer to the Lord, and accomplished more and had more joy while in the mission field than ever before or since. Man is that he may have joy, and the joy that I had in the mission field was superior to any I have ever experienced elsewhere. Get it into your hearts . . . to prepare yourselves to go out into the world where you can get on your knees and draw nearer to the Lord than in any other labor (*Gospel Standards,* 246).

There are so many souls who are lost—who simply need to be found. We are the finders. We are the seekers of those who know not God. "For there are many yet on the earth among all sects, parties, and denominations, who are blinded . . . and who are only kept from the truth because they know not where to find it" (D&C 123:12).

Elder LeGrand Richards related a story exemplifying this point:

> When I was president of the Hollywood Stake in California we converted a very prominent attorney down there. In one of our conferences I asked him if he would like to tell the people what he had found in Mormonism that appealed to him. He stood up and with a very rich, deep voice, he said, "If you have hunted for something all your life until you decided that it didn't exist, and then you just happened to stumble onto it, you do not need anybody to tell you that you have found it, do you?" He said, "That is what I did when I found Mormonism. The thing about it that is so wonderful to me is that the more I learn about it, the more wonderful it becomes" (BYU Speeches of the Year [1961], 6).

There are millions of our brothers and sisters who are just waiting for one of us to open our mouths and help them find the wonderful truths we almost take for granted. I recall a couple in our mission who decided to knock on doors. (Some consider this too scary and are not required to do it.) The Halversons did it. They found someone willing to listen who was converted and baptized. They saved someone's life. The question? What if they had not knocked on that door? They were instruments in the Lord's hand. He led them. They were obedient, and souls were saved in the kingdom of God. And you can bet that they will never forget the difference that simple act made—in their own lives, but also in the lives of generations to come.

## The Urgent Need for Senior Missionaries

Elder Hales spoke at April conference 2001 on the need for senior missionaries. He said, "I will speak on the *urgent need* for more mature couples to serve in the mission field. We wish to express our appreciation for all those valiant couples who are currently serving, those who have served, and those who will yet serve" (Robert D. Hales, "Couple Missionaries: A Time to Serve," *Ensign*, May 2001, 25). Why is there such an urgent need for couples and senior sisters? There are things that senior missionaries do that no one else is as qualified to do.

They can work with mature less-actives on a peer level. They provide leadership for the branches and wards they serve in. They have a lifetime of learning patience and charity behind them. I agree with Eldon C. McKell, president of the Alabama Birmingham Mission. He called couples "absolutely vital" to the success of his mission in some areas. "They take these little branches and hold them together," he said. "They bring stability, character, integrity and trust. Any mission president could use more couples." Elder Haight seconded the motion: "Mission presidents all over the world need the maturity, knowledge, and personal skills of retired couples to help strengthen their missions today just as much as we needed them in 1963. Couples add stability to a mission. They are role models for younger missionaries, and they offer mature thinking" (David B. Haight, "Couple Missionaries—'A Wonderful Resource,'"*Ensign*, Feb. 1996, 7). The list goes on and on in all the various aspects of missionary work. Believe me, you are needed in the mission field, for there is a work that only you can do.

When I served as mission president in England, we had one couple in the mission besides our two office couples. We had eight stakes, and we desperately needed one couple for each stake. I called the missionary department time and time again begging for senior missionaries. They expressed their sorrow for me, but there simply weren't any available. I knew that other missions had fifteen to twenty couples and wondered why I couldn't have just eight sets of senior missionaries. They said that they would try. I prayed and fasted, and one day an Apostle of the Lord came to our mission, Elder Russell M.

Nelson. We visited and he asked how he could help. I told him of my plight and he responded with, "I think I can help." And help he did. The Lord answered my prayers and we received eight couples and three sets of senior sisters in less than six months.

The work of those magnificent couples became legendary. They baptized, they reactivated, and they strengthened the new converts and blessed the lives of all the people in our mission. The young missionaries were blessed by their strengthening presence. Our family was blessed by their love. The stakes were rejuvenated and the wards had full-time help in leadership and member work. Most importantly the souls of our brothers and sisters were lifted and edified. Over a thousand people were reactivated and nearly a hundred were baptized because of their glorious service. And how hard was it to activate and baptize that many of their brothers and sisters? One couple said, "Oh President, this is so easy. It is just like being a home teacher or visiting teacher . . . and it is so much fun." Yep, it is fun to bless the lives of our brothers and sisters.

President Benson has admonished us to have more *fun*:

> We need increasing numbers of senior missionaries in missionary service. Where health and means make it possible, we call upon hundreds more of our couples to set their lives and affairs in order and to go on missions. How we need you in the mission field! You are able to perform missionary service in ways that our younger missionaries cannot.
>
> I'm grateful that two of my own widowed sisters were able to serve as missionary companions together in England. They were sixty-eight and seventy-three years of age when they were called, and they both had a marvelous experience.
>
> What an example and a blessing it is to a family's posterity when grandparents serve missions. Most senior couples who go are strengthened and revitalized by missionary service. Through this holy avenue of service, many are sanctified and feel the joy of bringing others to the knowledge of the fulness of the gospel of Jesus Christ.
>
> Also, through the Family-to-Family Book of Mormon Program, send copies of the Book of Mormon on missions for

you with your testimonies enclosed (Ezra Taft Benson, *Come Listen to a Prophet's Voice*, 74).

Couples who have answered this call to service couldn't agree more. Sister Loveless, who served in the Florida Jacksonville Mission after her husband's death, said, "There is so much need for the seniors in the Church to serve a mission. If you are inspired to fulfill a calling to go on a mission, don't hesitate, because your family is blessed because of it and so are you" ("The Service of Senior Missionaries Leads to Many New Friends to Love," *Church News,* 20 May 1995).

Sister Loveless is one of countless numbers who have seen what great things senior missionaries can do. The following is a wonderful arcticle on senior missionaries that Sarah Jane Weaver wrote for the *Church News:*

> Recently, a stake president reported to Pres. Terry J. Spallino of the England Birmingham Mission that a small branch within his stake boundaries needed something to help it grow.
>
> It needed, the stake president explained, a missionary couple. "The stake president said, 'If we can put a couple there to work with the young leadership and less-active members, we can meet our goals,'" Pres. Spallino recounted. "Couples have the ability to gain trust quickly. They are loved very quickly."
>
> Mission presidents around the world are receiving similar requests from local Church leaders who have witnessed the impact that couple missionaries—who bring years of experience, leadership, stability and strong testimonies into the mission field with them—can have on Church work.
>
> More than 1,600 couples are currently working in the mission field, but mission presidents and Church leaders say they "desperately need many, many more."
>
> The missionary department indicates many more couples are needed, especially now, when the number of couple missionaries in the Church is decreasing instead of increasing. At the present time there are hundreds of missionary assignments throughout the world that are not filled because there are not

enough couple missionaries being called to serve.

Couples who are in good health, with no permanent debilitating illnesses and who do not have dependent children at home, or are not in their childbearing years, can serve a mission for 12, 18 or 24 months.

The missionary department indicates a great need exists for couples who can help train local leaders, activate members, and fellowship new converts. Some couples serve in mission offices as secretaries, financial clerks, and vehicle coordinators. In addition, some couples are also needed to work in family history, public affairs, welfare, temples, Church education, and a variety of Church service assignments.

Quinn and Wilma Washburn decided in the 1950s that they would serve a mission when they were older. Today they are in Hong Kong, serving their third mission.

"We think every couple should serve a mission for their own benefit, as well as being able to help other people," they wrote in a letter to the Church News. "Most couples, because they have such wonderful experiences, have a great desire to go again—and sometimes again and again."

Troy and Marian Durtschi Butler of the Driggs 2nd Ward, Driggs Idaho Stake, are one of those couples. Currently in Quito, Ecuador, they have also served in Argentina, as well as in other South American countries. Sister Butler, who worked as a nurse before entering the mission field, said she feels indebted to the Lord for all He has given her and wants to show her gratitude.

Today, she is assisting the mission president's wife in handling common medical problems, such as colds and flus. In this assignment, her training as a nurse is useful. . . .

Colleen Asplund, Laramie (Wyo.) 1st Ward, who is serving a full-time mission with her husband, Owen, at historic Nauvoo, Ill., agrees.

"There are times when we get very lonesome for our family," she said, [but then] adding that her missionary experience— explaining Church history sites and participating in a nightly musical performance for visitors—has been a highlight in her life.

Elder Asplund agreed. "It has been a wonderful, wonderful experience," he said. "We have, for the first time in our life, spent 24 hours a day, seven days a week together. We have learned so much. We have had the opportunity here to study history and journals. . . ."

Noel Burt, president of the Connecticut Hartford Mission, said couple missionaries not only keep small areas of his mission running, but they also keep the mission office running. "They comment, 'We are here to serve the elders and sisters so that they can do a better job.' They do just that," he said. "They work their hearts out" ("Missionary Couples Fill Variety of Roles in Furthering Lord's Work," *Church News,* 14 Sept. 1996).

## A Commandment to "Work Our Hearts Out"

The Lord, referring among other things to missionary work, has asked that we "waste and wear out our lives in bringing to light all the hidden things of darkness" (D&C 123:13). And that commandment is not without a greater blessing, for He has also said that "whoso layeth down his life in my cause, for my name's sake, shall find it again, even life eternal" (D&C 98:13). In asking us to consecrate our lives to the building up of His kingdom, nothing has been more clear than the commandment to take the gospel to all mankind. "For behold, thus said Jesus Christ, the Son of God, unto his disciples who should tarry, yea, and also to *all his disciples,* in the hearing of the multitude: Go ye into *all the world,* and preach the gospel to every creature" (Morm. 9:22). Everyone needs to hear the gospel of Jesus Christ. Everyone needs to be nourished and strengthened by the good word of God.

Brother and Sister Jacobs took this scripture in Mormon literally and sought to teach all over the world. They were first assigned to the Eastbourne Branch in England. They strengthened the members, brought less-active members back, and baptized more members of a part-member family. And when they returned home from England, they continued to preach and teach, and I had the joy of witnessing the baptism of two of their friends from England here in Provo. They freely made their life a mission for the Lord. They have been back to England on their own to nourish their friends. Recently they returned from a mission to China where they taught English as a second language. Yes, they have gone into all the world and fulfilled the words of Matthew: "Go ye therefore, and teach all nations, baptizing them in the name of the Father, and of the Son, and of the Holy Ghost" (Matt. 28:19).

What made Brother and Sister Jacobs such a force for good? Just living the gospel, and thereby loving it and wanting to share. The Lord admonished Peter to do the same, "But I have prayed for thee, that thy faith fail not: and when thou art converted, strengthen thy brethren" (Luke 22:32). You do not need to be the prophet to go out and teach with conviction—all you need is to love the gospel, to live it, and to have the desire to share it.

It has been my experience that senior missionaries simply radiate their love for the people and for the joy of teaching—nourishing people in the word of God. Every month as a mission president I invited senior missionaries to our home for a "couples' meeting." They each stood and reported their stewardship. They were spotless and blameless, and they were full of joy in the work of the Lord. They expressed their weakness and dependence on the Lord in the work, thus fulfilling the words in the Doctrine and Covenants: "That the fulness of my gospel might be proclaimed by the weak and the simple unto the ends of the world, and before kings and rulers" (D&C 1:23).

They proved Ether's words that in their weakness they would be humbled and the Lord would make them strong (see Ether 12:27). They were a part of the "marvelous work [that is coming] forth among the children of men" (D&C 4:1).

Senior missionaries are now all over the earth. They serve on every continent. They often go as a lead couple to prepare the way for a nation or area to receive the proselyting effort. They are like angels. Just as the angel Moroni prepared the Prophet, so will you be even like unto angels of God preparing the way and assisting in the work.

> "And ye shall go forth in the power of my Spirit, preaching
> my gospel, two by two, in my name, lifting up your voices as
> with the sound of a trump, declaring my word like unto angels

of God" (D&C 42:6).

But you can't be someone's missionary angel until you put in your mission papers, and then the Lord through His prophets will assign you to the place where you can bless lives. "And how shall they preach, except they be sent? as it is written, How beautiful are the feet of them that preach the gospel of peace, and bring glad tidings of good things!" (Rom. 10:15). You first agree to do His will, just as Christ did the will of the Father, and then you can be an instrument for good in the Lord's hands. And yes, the feet of them that bring good tidings, that preach the gospel and bring souls to Christ are beautiful, and you shall be blessed.

And the converse is true if we fail to preach His gospel—we will lose out on the most beautiful gifts Heavenly Father can give us: "For though I preach the gospel, I have nothing to glory of: for necessity is laid upon me; yea, *woe is unto me,* if I preach not the gospel!" (1 Cor. 9:16). This scripture is not to produce guilt, but rather to teach the urgency and importance of the work.

Jacob, as a teacher and prophet and scribe in the Book of Mormon, records the importance of teaching the gospel:

> And we did magnify our office unto the Lord, taking upon us the responsibility, answering the sins of the people upon our own heads if we did not teach them the word of God with all diligence; wherefore, by laboring with our might their blood might not come upon our garments; otherwise their blood would come upon our garments, and we would not be found spotless at the last day (Jacob 1:19).

Jacob is teaching an important principle about stewardship. And just as we don't want the responsibility of others' sins on our hands, we all probably want to have our own sins forgotten. This is also a promised blessing: having our sins forgiven if we heed the Savior's call to feed His sheep.

### A Purifying Work

Missionary work is purifying work. We are forgiven of our sins as we bring souls to Christ. It is part of our own perfection process.

Note the following scriptures:

1. "For I will forgive you of your sins with this commandment—
   that you remain steadfast in your minds in solemnity and the
   spirit of prayer, in bearing testimony to all the world of those
   things which are communicated unto you" (D&C 84:61).

2. "Therefore, thrust in your sickle with all your soul, and your
   sins are forgiven you, and you shall be laden with sheaves
   upon your back, for the laborer is worthy of his hire.
   Wherefore, your family shall live" (D&C 31:5).

3. "And verily mine eyes are upon those who have not as yet
   gone up unto the land of Zion; wherefore your mission is not
   yet full. Nevertheless, ye are blessed, for the testimony which
   ye have borne is recorded in heaven for the angels to look
   upon; and they rejoice over you, and your sins are forgiven
   you" (D&C 62:2–3).

4. "Let him know, that he which converteth the sinner from the
   error of his way shall save a soul from death, and shall hide a
   multitude of sins" (James 5:20).

Is it any wonder that Jacob records that they labored with "all dili-
gence" (see 5:74) and admonishes us to do the same, "wherefore, by
laboring with our might" (see 1:19) we might see the removal of our
own sins. If nothing else, for this reason alone we should desire to
work our hearts out in spreading the gospel of peace and joy.

## The Blessings of Sacrifice

Some days as I teach the senior missionaries I get teary-eyed real-
izing the sacrifice they are making, and at the same time I feel almost
envious of the joy they will experience as full-time missionaries. They
will experience joy as their hearts swell with love, for sacrifice is built
on love. One must first build upon the principle of love and selfless-

ness if one is to participate in authentic sacrifice. Without love, there can be no willing and genuine sacrifice. One can be deprived of possessions, life, limb, and liberty; but only when one willingly gives up these things for a cause can one be said to have "sacrificed."

Elder Hales explains that we should willingly sacrifice out of gratitude for our blessings, and as a sign of our dedication to our Savior and His cause:

> As Jesus sent forth the Twelve to go on their missions, He commanded them, saying, "Freely ye have received, freely give" (Matt. 10:8). Where much is given, much is expected. You have received much in your life; go forth and freely give in the service of our Lord and Savior. Have faith; the Lord knows where you are needed. The need is so great, brothers and sisters, and the laborers are so few (*Ensign*, May 2001, 27).

Sacrifice is a measure of commitment. If one is committed to the well-being of one's family, community, or country, then no sacrifice is too great in achieving that goal. And especially when that goal is the forwarding of God's eternal plans for our happiness.

Sacrifice is a wholesome experience because it puts things in perspective. Worldly goods pale in value next to enduring relationships and spiritual well-being. We need to sacrifice for things that will bless others. The greatest joy comes in service to others. We need to sacrifice the "now" pleasures for the "later" benefits in life. We receive inner strength through sacrifice. President Gordon B. Hinckley has said, "Sacrifice is the very essence of religion; it is the keynote of a happy home life, the basis of true friendship, the foundation of peaceful community living, of sound relations among people and nations" (*Without Sacrifice There Is No True Worship*, BYU Speeches of the Year [1962], 1).

President Kimball has counseled us concerning our responsibility to sacrifice. He said:

> Again I am impressed to ask anew the question—is each of us doing all we can to take the gospel to the inhabitants of the

earth whom the Lord has placed within our circle of influence? There is an urgency about this work that I feel some have not sensed, but it is an urgency in the soul of each person who asks God for help in these matters. The Lord has advised us, "For if you will that I give unto you a place in the celestial world, you must prepare yourselves by doing the things which I have commanded you and required of you" (D&C 78:7). Is there in the Church today anyone who knows not the call of the Lord for "every member to be a missionary?" Is there any family in the Church today that knows not the need for more missionaries?

I wish we could more effectively and faithfully establish in the hearts of all members of the Church the understanding that if a person is old enough to be a member, he is old enough to be a missionary; and he doesn't need to be set apart especially for that calling. Every member has the obligation and the calling to take the gospel to those around him. We want every man, woman, and child to assume [their] rightful responsibility. It is very important. For this is the message of the gospel: We receive blessings from the gospel, and then we go out and share those blessings with others.

Now, we are a busy people; but the Lord did not say, "If it is convenient for you, would you consider preaching the gospel." He has said, "Let every man learn his duty" (D&C 107:99). . . . We must come to think of our obligation rather than our convenience. The time, I think, is here when sacrifice must become an even more important element in the Church. I feel the Lord has placed, in a very natural way within our circles of friends and acquaintances, many persons who are ready to enter into his Church. We ask that you prayerfully identify those persons and then ask the Lord's assistance in helping you introduce them to the gospel (Spencer W. Kimball, "Are We Doing All We Can?" *Ensign*, Feb. 1993, 3).

A senior sister wrote me this letter about the refining influence of sacrifice—the blessing end of the commandment.

I wish to speak of the outstanding men and women with whom I have associated on a daily basis these past two and a half months. They truly stand as "Beacons of Righteousness." I have come to know these are not couples and single sisters who are in the peak of health or have total financial security. But rather many come as the lame and the poor—many selling homes to be here; many with heavy burdens, whose needs are known only unto God. As I walked to my room one morning, I glanced into rooms as I passed. Medicine and prescription bottles lined nearly every table I passed. By the time I reached my room, I paused and said quietly to my Father in Heaven, "These are some of the finest brethren and sisters on the earth. They are my heroes!" I was grateful for His giving me an unspoken insight into sacred consecration.

We have seen many couples come and go. All are filled with missionary zeal and an excitement to perform the Lord's work. When we arrived here in February, we met a gentleman and his wife in their mid-eighties. They were about to embark on their eighth mission. They were learning Spanish, preparing to serve in South America. I have seen two blind men accompanied by their wives. I have viewed one totally deaf gentleman. He and his wife will serve in Australia. Our last mission we became dear friends with two couples. One where the brother had suffered a stroke and was left partially paralyzed. His wife assisted him in dressing each morning. His countenance beamed and he was an example to us all. The other brother was aided with an oxygen tank. One other brother in our group at that time could neither read nor write. He and his wife left to serve in Philadelphia where they would microfilm old court records. He was so delighted that the Lord could use him and told us that often. Today I visited with a single sister preparing to go to Puerto Rico. She has had cancer three times, and just three months ago had one kidney removed. She told me, "I already had my papers in, so I just asked the Lord to please heal me quickly, and here I am!" What an amazing sister! What a testimony builder!

—Senior Sister, MTC, 2001

Elder Holland has encouraged us with a similar testimony to the ennobling nature of sacrifice:

> Now let me increase the tempo of this message just a little. Many more of us can prepare for senior missionary service when that time in our life comes. As the senior couples at the MTC in Provo have said on a poster, "Let's lengthen our shuffle!" I just returned from a long trip which took me to half a dozen missions. Everywhere I went during those weeks, I found senior couples giving the most remarkable and rewarding leadership imaginable, providing stability, maturity, and experience that no 19-year-old or 21-year-old could possibly be expected to provide. I found all kinds of couples, including a few former mission and temple presidents and their wives, who had come to parts of the world totally unknown to them to quietly, selflessly serve a second or a third or a fourth mission. I was deeply moved by every one of those people (*Ensign,* May 2001, 15).

A sister from Canada expressed her desire to sacrifice for the Lord and the blessings she received for doing so:

> In the early spring of 2000 our ward [the Lethbridge 1st Ward] had a special "missionary meeting." We as members were requested to "pray for a missionary experience." It was a great meeting and Clifford and I were inspired to follow the Brethren's counsel. We prayed to have a missionary experience. Clifford was turning 62 and we wanted to retire, but what would we do? We decided to go to the temple [Cardston Alberta Temple] to pray to see what we should do. We also continued our prayers at home for a "missionary experience"—never thinking to connect the two. We had saved for our retirement, but to retire we needed to sell our lake property. We had tried, but weren't successful. We had gone to the temple for several weeks. I will never forget the afternoon we left the temple and were driving home. I will always remember the exact place we were on the highway when Clifford turned to me and asked, "Well, did you get the answer I did?" "No," I said, but I immediately knew what he was going to say: "I

think we should sell our home and go on a mission." My stomach sank. I love my home in Lethbridge—I didn't want to leave it, but I also knew it was the thing we had to do. "Okay," I said.

We put our home up on the market. It was the first part of November 2000. We wanted to put it up for sale early because the house had sat vacant for two years before we bought it. Can you imagine our surprise when we had an offer in two days for $21,000.00 more than we had paid for it? We were then on the slippery slope. We had talked to our bishop, and before we had even sat down in his office he knew why we were there. Our papers went in quickly and we were called to the Ghana Accra Mission. But we weren't to be in the mission home until April 3, 2001. We had to be out of our house by December 15, 2000. All our belongings were put into storage. Where would we live? Again the Lord blessed us—a house was available for just payment of the utilities. "House-sitting" they called it. "Please use the linen, the food in the fridge and in the cupboard," they said—and so we did.

All we have to do is to put our faith in Heavenly Father. We know that our missionary experience is probably not unique, but it is ours and it is special. Because we are insurance investigators, we have many people [we know] who are not members of the Church, but they were all so happy for us, and I know they have also had a missionary experience. Many of them came to our farewell. One friend, Harrison Wolf Child, I will never forget calls me the "Mormon Squaw Adjuster." We touch people's lives whether we want to or not. We will either "be an example or be made an example of." One nonmember friend jokingly said, "You Mormons are goofy. Why, they call you to some foreign place and you immediately pack your suitcase and go?" He said it with admiration in his eyes. Many of our nonmember friends openly wept when we bore our testimonies at our farewell.

In the MTC they have said that "it might be hard being with your husband for 24 hours." I have been with my husband for 24 hours for a long time. I have worked alongside two young men who are my sons every day, and if I want to be with them for eternity, we had better practice here on earth. This is the

Lord's work and I am so happy to be a part of it. Now once our visas arrive we will be off to Ghana, West Africa.

—Elder and Sister Noble

Elder and Sister Samuel and Antoinette Makanoa are from Kaneohe on the island of Oahu in the Hawaiian Islands. They have five children, three of whom served missions. The other two have served stake missions with their husbands. They must have learned the blessings of sacrifice, because they just keep doing it.

When our last son came back from his mission, we announced to our family that it would be our turn now. We put in our papers, and we decided at that time that we would serve five missions.

In 1992 we had our first call to the Phillippines Ilagan Mission. We had to adjust to the excessive heat, myriad insects, doing everything by hand, pumping our own water, and getting along without electricity much of the time. The area where we were located was quite rural and primitive, so we tried to live like the natives, forgetting ourselves and loving the people. Doing so brought us closer to the Lord and we were able to love them like our own, so much that we wanted to go on another mission.

The next time we asked for the Philippines San Pablo Mission. We spent 11 months on Marinduque and then 13 months on Mindoro. The two missions were totally different. Our mission president said to us, "There's one place that I am not going to send any senior missionaries." It was an island and very primitive. No couples had been there before, only elders. And, of course, that is where we went. It was much more primitive than the first mission, but we made it so beautiful. We learned everybody's name on the island. We had the mission president and General Authorities come to visit us. We were like the parents for all the elders who were serving there. I felt like they were my own children.

For the third mission we asked President Banks if he would let us do a short mission, so we did a one-year family history mission, and we opened up family history centers in the Philippines.

For the fourth mission we served at the Missionary Reception Center in Manila. This is where the missionaries go when they first arrive and also where they go just before they are released to go home. Also when a missionary is sick, he/she is transferred to the Missionary Reception Center.

Our fifth mission was serving as managers of the Temple Patron Housing in Manila.

For our sixth mission we were called by President Gerrard to serve a two-month medical mission in the Philippines. There is a lot of tuberculosis in the Philippines, and the Church decided they should have their own x-ray machine, so we went around to the different missions and did all the x-raying.

Now, for our seventh mission we are going to serve in the Philippines Naga Mission for 18 months. We will be working with the district leaders to assist in turning districts into stakes.

After our second mission, our children complained a bit, but we reminded them that in the temple we covenant to give ourselves totally to the Lord and His work, and now they just accept our mission calls and ask when they can expect us to return next. We have been so blessed.

People have always asked us how we can afford to go on so many missions. When we first served in the Philippines, we learned that money and things are not important. I keep telling my husband the money we have is not ours anyway. It is the Lord's, and we are his stewards. We have enough with our Social Security and retirement.

## Conclusion

The Lord is aware of all His children's needs. He knows our concerns and our fears, and He knows what we need better than we do. When we sacrifice for Him, He pours down blessings from heaven. "Prove me now herewith, saith the Lord of Hosts, if I will not open you the windows of heaven, and pour you out a blessing that there shall not be room enough to receive it" (3 Ne. 24:10). Our fears should not keep us from showing the Lord our commitment and gratitude. If we find ourselves afraid to serve, we should simply follow our prophet's reassuring words as relayed by Carol Thomas, counselor in the Young Women's General Presidency:

> Recently President Hinckley visited a stake conference in an affluent area where only four older couples were serving missions. Hoping to inspire more members to serve, he promised them that their children and grandchildren would not even miss them while they're gone. With the invention of e-mail, friendly letters can be sent and received by senior missionaries just about any day.
>
> Your years of experience will bless others, and you'll discover how wonderful people really are. The missions of the world need you! Pray for that spirit of adventure and a desire to serve a mission. You'll enjoy more excitement than motor home travel or rocking chairs ("Sacrifice: An Eternal Investment," *Ensign*, May 2001, 64).

Yes, building up the kingdom of God requires that our rocking chairs sit vacant a few more years, but we are truly needed like never before in the history of the Church. The wonderful part is that you are prepared: you are available and you love the Lord. All you have to do is to take the step—visit with the bishop, put your missionary papers in, and trust in the Lord—and your hearts will be full as you serve your Savior and Father in Heaven: you will know and feel the purpose and the joy of missionary work!

# CHAPTER 2

## BEING READY AND WILLING TO SERVE

With the urgent need for senior missionaries we must do all in our power to serve and encourage others to serve. This united effort to increase service in the Church worldwide will create the force for good we need to welcome more of God's children into the fold, and most importantly to build our own spirituality, charity, and unity as a people—moving us boldly toward the goal of Zion.

## Getting Senior Missionaries in the Field

We should all be ready and willing to serve and to help others serve. The following sections outline several things we can do as a united Church body, and as individuals, to help us move the great cause of missionary work forward.

### Priesthood Leaders Can Encourage

Elder Robert D. Hales recounts what our prophets have asked of priesthood leaders concerning the need for more missionaries: "Bishops, there should be no hesitation on your part to initiate a Recommend for Missionary Service interview to discuss and encourage missionary couples to serve a mission" (*Ensign*, May 2001, 27). Bishops do have a responsibility to watch over their flocks, and keeping the flock spiritually growing and building the kingdom of God is part of that responsibility.

President Ezra T. Benson stated that there are many types of missions bishops can offer—the important point is just to encourage service.

> A priesthood leader can do much to assist and encourage individuals and couples as they prepare to serve missions. The temple extraction and welfare programs are blessed greatly by those who are in their senior years and have opportunities to serve in this area (*Come, Listen to a Prophet's Voice,* 71).

Elder David B. Haight gave instructions on how to deal with this responsibility constructively and with sensitivity:

> When in doubt, it is the bishop's responsibility to suggest to couples that they think about going on a mission. He ought to have a list on his desk of all those couples he thinks are eligible. He needs to know something about their family, health, and financial situations. Then he should call them in for a warm and friendly interview and say, "Now that you're retired, you have the opportunity to be doing something more to help build the kingdom. Have you ever thought about serving a mission?"
>
> We don't force anyone! We don't say you have to go! But we are saying that there is a need! Bishops can talk about the couple's possibility of going in six months or a year if the couple isn't ready to go right now. It doesn't have to happen overnight; the need of the Church is ongoing.
>
> I think that some bishops are a little reluctant to bring up the idea of a mission to some couples because they are not sure of all the details in a couple's life. In that case, a couple should go to the bishop and say, "We're ready!"
>
> We need to improve communication from both directions, but it is ultimately the bishop's responsibility to at least raise the question (*Ensign,* Feb. 1996, 7).

### Other Couples Can Encourage

There are thousands of couples and senior sisters just waiting for an invitation to serve or an encouraging word about serving a mission. You as individuals can go to your priesthood and auxiliary leaders and promote a "Let's go on a mission campaign." Your word could be what starts someone else's desire to serve. The results: many lives are blessed in the mission field, your families at home will be blessed, and you will feel the joy of assisting the Lord by serving others, and helping them to serve their fellowmen. Encouragement from others really helps.

A senior missionary explains how encouragement helped her:

> One of the things that has given me the courage to dare tackle a mission is when my cousin's husband told us that we should serve a mission. We told him that we really weren't missionary material, and he told us that we would be very surprised at what we could do. He said that we very well could know more about the Church than many members in the mission field, maybe even the stake president. Our prayers have been that we can and will be of use in the Palmyra area. We are excited to do this—share what we know and are learning of this wonderful gospel.
>
> —Sister Higbee

## Getting the Word Out

Following are some ideas to encourage senior missionary service. They should be ongoing so younger members can also build up their desire to serve. If we do so, we can all help encourage and plant the seed of desire in the hearts of all the members of the Church. When the time comes, the decision is already made and the price of preparation has been paid. Then we are ready to serve the Lord as senior missionaries.

1. Have a joint priesthood/Relief Society fireside or Sunday School class to help members to gain a desire and be aware of the opportunities to serve in all types of missionary activities.

2. Alleviate fear by having returned senior missionaries talk at firesides or in classes and explain how they overcame their fear. (See chapter six for examples of such stories.)

3. Have a missionary month with emphasis on setting a date to serve. It could include sacrament meetings, firesides, workshops (covering types of missionary service, preparing to serve, etc.).

4. Make a list of all possible and available seniors who could serve. Sometimes people just need to be asked to serve.

5. Prepare a handout for all those who could serve with statements by the prophets and others which could inspire them to serve.

6. Review the weekly missionary bulletin in all appropriate meetings to remind people that they are desperately needed.

7. Always use the ward bulletin and newsletter to encourage missionary service, and include success stories of senior missionaries.

## Initiating the Call

We should always be anxiously engaged in a good cause (see D&C 58: 27). And missionary work is the greatest cause I know. It embraces all aspects of life, for in bringing souls to Christ we become saviors to the world. We assist the Lord in His great work. The wonderful part about this work is that we can initiate the call—we can volunteer to serve the Lord and our fellowmen. We never need to wait to be asked.

Elder Haight has encouraged the senior couples to serve. He said:

> [Couples who want to go on a mission] ought to pray and talk to the Lord about it. They hopefully do understand that the purpose of the Church is to carry to all people the message that God lives, that Jesus is the promised Christ and Redeemer, and that this is the church that the Lord has restored to earth in the latter days through the Prophet Joseph Smith. Potential couple missionaries should feel the importance of a mission and feel that they can make a contribution.

Then couples need to review their family, health, and financial situations. If they feel that things are in place and if their bishop has not talked to them yet, they should go to their bishop and say, "Bishop, we think it's time to talk about our going on a mission. . . ." The bishop will be thrilled and can take care of everything from there.

The Brethren hope that many, many more couples will make themselves available for full-time service to the Church. The need is great! Hundreds of thousands of new members join the Church each year, and they need to hear a friendly voice of support and comfort from experienced members.

The refrain, "I'll go where you want me to go, dear Lord" (*Hymns,* 1985, no. 270), should be more than a hymn we sing on Sunday. It should be our own prayer of faith as we serve wherever the Lord has need of us (*Ensign,* Feb. 1996, 7).

When asked who initiated their mission call, one senior missionary couple responded, "If we had waited for our bishop to initiate the call we would still be sitting at home. We went in and told him we were ready to go." Another couple offered, "For the last ten years this has been a goal for when we retired." From a couple possibly more timid: "Our branch president was very encouraging and supported us in the knowledge that we would be blessed, our family would be blessed, and our branch president would be blessed. And we hope to bless others with the gospel of Jesus Christ on our mission." And simply but gloriously put, "We met with the bishop and told him we would like to serve a mission."

## Preparing Yourself

Now to making our own decision to serve. We all know it's much easier to do something (especially something we *think* is hard) when we've mentally prepared ourselves for it. And that's the goal of this book—to mentally prepare seniors to go, and not-yet-seniors to plan on it—long before any fears can set in. Resolve doesn't leave much room for fear.

## Deciding Early

We teach our children over and over to decide about important things early in life—attend seminary and institute, go to church, serve a mission, and get married in the temple. I remember as a father playing a game in family home evening. We called it "Decide Now for the Future." We wrote down on a piece of paper all the important decisions in life, from saying our prayers, searching the scriptures, attending church, and obeying the word of wisdom, to preparing to serve missions and being married in the temple. The children each evaluated the choices and made notes on their papers. They had then made a decision early which would bless their lives forever. Make the decision early. This takes all the pressure away because you've already decided. Tell your family and friends—make the decision and stick with it! Then you'll be eligible for blessings in advance, and it will inspire everyone to be missionaries for the Lord.

Elder Hales has said as much, asking couples to plan early for service and for the blessings that service will bring.

> To younger couples with children still at home, I urge you now to decide to serve [a mission] in your later years and to plan and prepare so you are financially, physically, and spiritually able. Make certain that the great example of missionary service is a heritage you will leave your posterity (*Ensign,* May 2001, 27).

A couple from the MTC related their positive experiences that resulted from planning early:

> My wife and I have had as a goal to serve a mission together for over 20 years. We retired from our job in St. Augustine, FL, on March 30th and reported to the Senior MTC on April 10, 2001.
>
> We have always wanted to share with other people the things that bring us so much joy and happiness, the gospel of Jesus Christ. We want to be able to serve as long as our health is okay. We are so happy to be here. We are now having the opportunity to teach the gospel to people we don't know, even though they are Church members. The Spirit is so strong during these lessons; it

makes me excited to get to the field and teach those less-active or part-member families whom the Lord has prepared for us.

We would like every couple in our age bracket to think seriously about missionary service. We don't want to be selfish and have all the fun and receive *all* the blessings promised for such service. Our lives have been so touched and [have] changed so much during our short stay at the MTC. Please tell others when you have the chance to please come here.

—Elder and Sister Udy

## *Evaluating and Planning*

The old adage "If you fail to plan, you plan to fail" is true. Planning to complete our goals is a key step toward success. One cannot underestimate the power of preparation through proper planning. Elder Hales again encourages us to evaluate our lives:

Sit down with your companion, make an inventory of your health, financial resources, and unique gifts and talents. Then, if all is in order, go to your bishop and say, "We're ready." You may feel it is improper to approach your bishop or branch president about your desire to serve a mission. But it is proper for a mature sister or couple to let their priesthood leaders know that they are willing and able to serve a mission. I urge you to do so (*Ensign,* May 2001, 27).

Here is a checklist of eight things to consider as you plan to serve a mission:

1. *Be specific:* Evaluate your situation and ask, "When can we serve?"

2. *Be flexible:* Plan from the outset to be resilient, flexible, accommodating, and willing to adjust.

3. *Be realistic, look to the future, and write it down:* Consider details like family relationships, concerns,

personal and family needs, and target dates. Plan for now and the distant future (setting aside funds now with a future date and other needs in mind).

4. *Plan together as a couple or with a friend:* People need to be involved in the planning process to both assist and encourage. Be sure that all who are part of the planning process understand the details and the goal in mind.

5. *Review often:* Planning is a process, not an event. Plan to review your plan frequently in order to keep it dynamic and alive.

6. *Have resources in place:* Arrange for all things and people to be in place, then there are no worries.

7. *Plan with a purpose:* Keep a focus on your goal. Be excited to reap the harvest of hard work and effort. Plan for a life of service and anticipate the blessings: lasting harmony, peace, togetherness, and joy.

8. *Plan for your happiness:* You can count on it— happiness for yourselves and those you serve.

A senior missionary related how planning to serve a mission made the dream come true, and how that choice enriched his life and increased his desire to serve:

> From the very beginning of our marriage my wife and I have planned to serve a mission together. Now our daughter (our last child) is in the MTC and we are fulfilling our dream. I love my Heavenly Father and my Savior and I want to demonstrate that love by helping others of His children to come back home. When I contemplate their incomprehensible sacrifice I feel a great need to give of myself to help make it effective in the lives of my brothers and sisters. How can I look upon the wounds of the Atonement

without shrinking if I have not given my best in His service? There is nothing to compare with the feeling here in the MTC.

We are so grateful for the opportunity of being here in the MTC preparing to go out on a mission. My wife and I are both on a second marriage. Since we were first married we made plans to serve a mission. In April 1990 we went to the MTC. While at the MTC we were together with four other couples. We were soon very close to each other and love flowed freely. We were the youngest couple. One lady, who was the eldest of our group, was 75 years of age. My wife admired this lady and told her that she hoped we could still go on missions when we reached her age. She responded, "Oh, Sister, they will take you as long as you can sit up and take nourishment." Her encouragement has inspired us to continue serving missions. We have been blessed with the health and energy to do so.

So far we have served two missions in Quebec, Canada; a two-year mission to Jamaica; and a mission to England. These were all microfilming missions.

We are very excited to serve this fifth mission to Cove Fort. This will be a new experience to share the gospel at a visitors' center.

We are so grateful for all the many people we have come in contact with. We love them all.

—Elder Gary Jespersen

We make plans for everything in life: education, vocation, marriage, and family. Even our hobbies and vacations are part of our planning. As Saints we need to make our plans to serve in our mature years.

The following couple recognized the blessings of missionary work and planned to serve even before their family was raised.

About thirty years ago we moved to a small branch and came in contact for the first time with senior missionary couples. As we saw them work with the members and grew to love them, we determined right then to serve in the same way when our family was raised.

We lived in other branches over the intervening years and had more experiences with couple missionaries. That strengthened our determination to serve. We saw the remarkable change that came over a young couple who had been excommunicated as the couple worked with them. We would not have believed the changes they made had we not been there.

We planned our lives so that we would be spiritually self-sufficient. We planned our retirement so we could have one year to recharge our batteries and be ready to serve at the same time as our youngest son. That worked perfectly and he entered the MTC one week before us.

—Sister Robyn Denley

We can organize every needful thing and set our date to talk to the bishop and tell him, "WE ARE READY!" What a joy to anticipate this time in our life. Like one senior sister at the MTC said, "Why should we let the young missionaries have all the fun?" She is right. Decide now to have some of the fun—make plans today for *your* mission.

### Living the Gospel Prepares You

Even if you haven't planned, you're still prepared! There's no getting out of it—even missing an opportunity to plan can't handicap you when you really get into the work of the Lord! You have the vision of the worth of souls. You are worthy and needed now! You are full of charity and merely need an opportunity to share it. This is what really makes you an instrument for good in the Lord's hands. Paul makes it very clear what counts for success in the kingdom of God:

Though I speak with the tongues of men and of angels, and have not charity, I am become as sounding brass, or a tinkling cymbal.

And though I have the gift of prophecy, and understand all mysteries, and all knowledge; and though I have all faith, so that I could remove mountains, and have not charity, I am nothing.

> And though I bestow all my goods to feed the poor, and
> though I give my body to be burned, and have not charity, it
> profiteth me nothing (1 Cor. 13:1–3).

You have learned charity by just living day to day—you have children and grandchildren, and I know raising them required that you
develop charity. You have close friends, spouses, relatives that love and
appreciate you, neighbors that speak highly of you. You have had
trials and tribulations, and from all of this you have learned charity.
And now is your chance to transfer that charity to the mission field—
where it is needed the most. Elder David B. Haight has stated:

> Charity is especially important in missionary work. Its influ-
> ence, radiated by the missionary, helps to create within the inves-
> tigator a desire to learn and softens his heart to the truth. Charity
> can fill the missionary with an unquenchable desire to serve his
> fellowmen. Without it, as difficulties arise and proselyting seems
> unfruitful, he may lose interest and slacken his pace. But with
> Christlike love, the missionary will persevere through adversity
> because he becomes a caring and dutiful messenger of Christ. A
> Christlike love for others can purify a missionary's motives and
> consecrate his labor and true desire to share the gospel (*A Light
> unto the World*, 73).

Yes, you know about charity. You are motivated in life and in all
righteous deeds because of love. You have loved God, your family, and
your fellowmen in countless acts of compassion and service. You
sisters have lived a life of charity, the pure love of Christ. You have
shown compassion in your families, in your wards, and in your
communities. As you think upon how love has given you a taste for
service, you can see how you have lived a life of love; and you can also
see how you have been blessed with love and service from others, and
how that has changed your life and prepared you for growth—just as
you can prepare others in the mission field through sharing your love.

But you have even more than charity; life has taught you more
than that. You have strong testimonies, interpersonal skills, and
gospel knowledge. Your testimonies are strong through years of

service and the bearing of them. You search the scriptures, fast and pray, and live by the Spirit. You have the wisdom of age. You are willing to work and sacrifice for your brothers and sisters. You have needed skills, and if necessary can make them better with practice. (Remember that the Lord will always bless those who are in His service.) You have the ability to make friends and build relationships of trust. Yes, you have had a lifetime of preparation. You are ready. If you are willing and available, you are prepared to receive a call to serve.

You need not fear; you have had the most important training you need. Your desire to serve and bless others has always been part of your life—as parents and members of the Church. Sometimes (just like when we deal with children) we feel like we are not strong enough or a good enough teacher. Remember that people respond to simple love. They want to be good as they feel the Spirit and your faith in them. You can strengthen them. "Therefore, strengthen your brethren in all your conversation, in all your prayers, in all your exhortations, and in all your doings" (D&C 108:7). That's what senior missionaries can do—and they do it so well because they've spent their lives strengthening their own testimonies and learning to love. Thousands of senior missionaries are needed because there are hundreds of thousands who need to be strengthened through their love and strong testimonies.

### Your Gospel Knowledge Prepares You

You are prepared. You know enough. Just look at all you know about the gospel of Jesus Christ! You have a great deal of knowledge. You have been visiting teachers and home teachers, Sunday School and auxiliary teachers; you have been parents to your children or the children and youth in the Church. You are teachers by precept and example. You may need to fine-tune some details or presentations, but you have enough knowledge to bless people's lives.

To prove my point, review the following pages to see how much you really do know about the six discussions. We'll start with a practice presentation of all the principles in the first discussion, and then simply touch on the principles for the other five discussions. It's a lot easier than you might think!

# 1) THE PLAN OF OUR HEAVENLY FATHER

The Plan of Happiness: Our Heavenly Father has a plan for our happiness. We believe in God the Eternal Father, his Son Jesus Christ, and the Holy Ghost. God, our Father, is perfect and knows all things. He, out of his love for us, made a plan that we might return to His presence if we but obey and keep his commandments. This plan of salvation is centered in His beloved Son, even the Lord Jesus Christ. Jesus is the Son of God and Savior of the world.

Jesus, the Divine Son of God: Christ overcame death and sin through His atoning sacrifice and the power of the resurrection. Jesus was sent to the earth to fulfill the magnificent Atonement. "Behold I have given unto you my gospel, and this is the gospel which I have given unto you—that I came into the world to do the will of my Father, because my Father sent me. And my Father sent me that I might be lifted up upon the cross; and after that I had been lifted up upon the cross, that I might draw all men unto me, that as I have been lifted up by men even so should men be lifted up by the Father, to stand before me, to be judged of their works, whether they be good or whether they be evil" (3 Ne. 27:13–14). God loved us so much that He gave us His only begotten son. And because of that, if we have faith in the Lord Jesus Christ, we can follow Him by keeping the commandments of the Lord and return to our Father in Heaven.

Revelation: Revelation is the key to knowing what we must do to return to God. God has followed this pattern throughout all times as He has taught His children here upon the earth. He chooses prophets who are witnesses for the Lord of eternal truths. These prophets testify of Christ, they testify of the goodness of God, they testify of the principles and ordinances of the gospel, they testify of all things that we are to do. And we are invited to obey and follow our prophets. "Surely the Lord God will do nothing, but he revealeth his secret unto his servants the prophets" (Amos 3:7). The plan of salvation is always keyed to living prophets—from Adam even down to the Prophet Joseph

Smith and to our present prophet, Gordon B. Hinckley. The Spirit testifies of this great truth and we should act upon this knowledge.

Joseph Smith, the Prophet of the Restoration: In our day the Lord followed the pattern of revelation and gave eternal truth to the Prophet Joseph Smith. As a young man, Joseph was concerned about which church to join. After reading James 1:5–6, he found that the Lord would answer his concerns. He sought to gain this knowledge. In the Sacred Grove Joseph prayed for wisdom and understanding of where truth was to be found, and he received a revelation. He saw God the Father and the Son. Joseph, after being told the full truth was no longer upon the earth, was then called to be the prophet of the Restoration and to be a witness that the Lord is in fact Jesus Christ.

The Book of Mormon: The Book of Mormon is the keystone of our religion. The Book of Mormon is another testament of the Lord Jesus Christ, and men will get closer to God by adhering to its principles than any other book (see the introduction to the Book of Mormon). Joseph Smith, through the power and authority of God, brought forth and translated the Book of Mormon. The Book of Mormon has brought forth the restoration of the full gospel in printed form. The Book of Mormon is a record of the dealings of our Heavenly Father and our Savior with the people on the American continent. It is the key for our coming unto Christ and being rooted in Him. It will lead us through temptation. It will continue to convert us as we daily search for ways to stay strong in the kingdom. As we seek to understand the Book of Mormon and make a commitment to read it, we will be blessed.

The Holy Ghost: The Holy Ghost confirms the truth of all things (see Moro. 10:5). We can know that God is our Father, Jesus is the Christ, Joseph Smith was a prophet, and that the Book of Mormon is true by the power of the Holy Ghost. It is important that we pray to gain a testimony of what we read and ponder. And as we pray to know these things are true, the Holy Ghost will show us that they are (see 2 Ne. 32:5).

There now, that wasn't so bad after all, was it? The rest of the discussions are just as easy to present, just like when you taught your kids or visit taught or home taught—second nature. They are outlined below with just a line or two defining each principle, just to give you an idea of what they cover.

## 2) THE GOSPEL OF JESUS CHRIST

Salvation from Physical Death: The gospel of Jesus Christ is the foundation of the Church. Salvation and eternal life come as we conquer both death and sin . . .

Salvation from Sin: We have been given agency—the right to choose. When we go against God and His will we sin, thus separating ourselves from God . . . We can be forgiven and restored if we repent. To do this, we must apply the first four principles and ordinances of the gospel:

1. *Faith:* Faith in the Lord Jesus Christ is the first principle of the gospel. Faith is hope and belief. Faith is the moving cause of all action. Faith is the power to do all things. It is in fact the vehicle of the priesthood, the power by which the earth was created . . .

2. *Repentance:* Repentance is the second principle of the gospel. We are not perfect, but we can become perfect through the principle of repentance—by repenting perfectly . . .

3. *Baptism:* The third principle of the gospel is baptism. We make a covenant with the Lord that we will take His name upon us, that we will keep His commandments, and that we will follow Him. Baptism is a symbol of death, burial, and resurrection . . .

4.  *The Holy Ghost:* The Holy Ghost is the most priceless gift one can receive here upon the earth in order to return to our Heavenly Father's presence. The Holy Ghost will lead, guide, direct, support, sustain, and comfort us in all things . . .

Enduring to the End and Keeping the Commandments of God: Obedience is the first law of heaven. If we endure to the end in obedience, we shall be blessed. All blessings are predicated on obedience to the law (see D&C 130:19–21) . . .

## 3) THE RESTORATION OF THE CHURCH AND KINGDOM OF GOD:

We Must Be Seekers of Truth: We must seek our Heavenly Father and His knowledge, for man has limited knowledge . . .

The Great Apostasy: A falling away occurred following the death of the apostles of the Lord Jesus Christ, and priesthood authority was lost . . .

Required Restoration of Truth: God revealed His lost truths to the Prophet Joseph Smith . . .

The Restoration of the Church: Before the Church could be restored, we first had to have the gospel of Jesus Christ. That was brought forth by the power of the Book of Mormon. Next, the priesthood had to be restored . . . Through the priesthood, gospel ordinances can be preformed. And then the Church, the vehicle of the Lord to help us return to His presence, was reestablished . . .

Membership in the True Church: We come unto Christ by belonging to His church. Membership in the church is key to our commitment to the Lord by taking upon us His name . . .

Attending Church Meetings and Renewing Our Covenants: We are taught that we are to meet together oft. "And the church did meet together oft, to fast and to pray, and to speak one with another concerning the welfare of their souls. And they did meet together oft to partake of the bread and wine, in remembrance of the Lord Jesus" (Moro. 6:5–6) . . .

# 4) ETERNAL PROGRESSION:

Premortal Existence: We lived before our mortal birth with our Heavenly Father. He taught us His plan. We, as His children, accepted that plan to come here to earth . . .

Mortal Life: Life here on earth has a purpose. We have a physical body that we must learn to tame and to direct as we make correct choices as inspired by the Spirit . . .

Life after Death: Death is part of the plan of our Heavenly Father. Death is but birth to life eternal. Our spirits will go to the spirit world, and then later we will be resurrected and judged . . .

Redeeming the Dead: Many die without the gospel of Jesus Christ. The gospel is taught in the spirit world. We learn this from 1 Peter 3:18–19; 4:6 . . . We perform baptisms for the dead (see 1 Cor. 15:29). These are performed in the temple of our God . . .

The Eternal Family: Here on the earth we have the power of procreation. This is a sacred power that helps us create families. Families can be eternal and need not end in death . . .

The Law of Chastity: Procreation is so sacred that we must not only bridle our passions, but abstain from any sexual relations outside of wedlock. God's power to create must be governed . . .

The Word of Wisdom: Our bodies are sacred. They are temples of our spirits. We should avoid all harmful materials that can be taken into our bodies . . .

## 5) LIVING A CHRISTLIKE LIFE

The purpose of existence here upon the earth is to become even as He is—even as the Lord Jesus Christ (see 3 Ne. 27:27). We are to be full of love and seek the interest of our fellowmen and their happiness.

The Two Great Commandments: God gave us two great commandments—to love the Lord thy God and to love all mankind . . .

Sacrifice Brings Forth Blessings: We must learn to sacrifice our own interests in behalf of our God, our Savior, and our fellowmen . . .

Fasting and Fast Offerings: The Lord has given us a commandment to fast. Through fasting we become selfless and pure. We also fast so that we can give blessings to those who are less fortunate. We fast each month and set aside that money we would have used on food to bless the poor . . .

Tithing: "Will a man rob God?" We learn in Malachi 3:8–11 that we can rob God if we fail to pay our tithing . . .

## 6) MEMBERSHIP IN THE KINGDOM OF GOD:

The Lord Jesus Christ in the Plan of Salvation: As we take upon ourselves the name of the Lord Jesus Christ, we become members of His kingdom here upon the earth . . .

<u>Exaltation Comes In and Through the Lord Jesus Christ:</u>
Exaltation is the greatest gift of God. "And, if you keep my commandments and endure to the end you shall have eternal life, which gift is the greatest of all the gifts of God" (D&C 14:7) . . .

<u>The Threefold Mission of the Church:</u>

1. *Perfecting the Saints:* We work for the salvation of others. We perfect the saints. This is what the Church is for—to help perfect the saints as we hear the word of God and then live the word of God . . .

2. *Proclaiming the Gospel:* It is our duty to proclaim the gospel. Many are kept from the truth, for they know not where to find it (see D&C 123:12) . . .

3. *Redeeming the Dead:* The temples of our God were established for the blessings of the people here upon the earth and for those who have gone on to the spirit world. It is in the temples of our God that we do vicarious work, that we truly become saviors of mankind (see D&C 103:9–10) . . .

<u>The Strait and Narrow Way:</u> We have learned that after we have been baptized we must continue on the strait and narrow path to return to the presence of our Heavenly Father (see Matt. 7:13–14) . . .

We're done! You could have just given the six discussions—and just think . . . you knew it all. See, you really are prepared; you have the knowledge. The question is, are you willing to serve the Lord now?

## Will You Go and Do?

Desire is often called the mother of change. It is the motivation from within. The question in life is: How do you create righteous desires? How do you keep your righteous desires alive? Apathy destroys desire, but true love and a vision of life's purpose keep desire alive. When understood and appreciated, the love of God and truth, and a vision of the work and of the worth of souls will create desire in our hearts to serve missions.

In his October 2001 conference address, Elder Dallin H. Oaks addressed the topic of creating a desire to serve. He asserted the following:

> If we are to become more effective instruments in the hands of the Lord in sharing His gospel, we must sincerely *desire* to do so. I believe we acquire this desire in two steps.
>
> First, we must have a firm testimony of the truth and importance of the restored gospel of Jesus Christ. This includes the supreme value of God's plan for His children, the essential position of the Atonement of Jesus Christ in it, and the role of The Church of Jesus Christ in carrying out that plan in mortality.
>
> Second, we must have a love for God and for all of His children. In modern revelation we are told that "love, with an eye single to the glory of God, qualifies [us] for the work" (D&C 4:5). The early Apostles of this dispensation were told that their love should "abound unto all men" (D&C 112:11).
>
> From our testimony of the truth and importance of the restored gospel, we understand the value of what we have been given. From our love of God and our fellowmen, we acquire our desire to share that great gift with everyone. The intensity of our desire to share the gospel is a great indicator of the extent of our personal conversion ("Sharing the Gospel," *Ensign,* Nov. 2001, 7).

Take an inventory of your life. What are your convictions—what parts of your gospel knowledge or testimony would you like to bolster? How much do you love truth? What do you want to have happen in your future? What do you enjoy and why? From these questions make a list of righteous and positive desires. Recognize the value of each good desire and prioritize the desires so that you can focus most on those that will help build up the kingdom (see JST—Matt 6:38). Surround yourself with objects that remind you of positive goals. Think positive thoughts, pray for positive thoughts, say positive things, sing positive songs, make positive plans, and be with positive people. The Lord needs you. Keeping the desire alive is as important as generating the desire in the first place. Have a clear view of the positive outcomes of your good desires, and remember all the good that comes from serving God and your fellowmen.

One sister describes how learning truth led her to love it, and how that love led to a desire to leave everything behind and serve over and over and over again.

I really had no concerns about coming on another mission. When I heard the message of the restored gospel thirty-five years ago, I was so thrilled that I joined the Church within two weeks of my first discussion. I started dejunking my life of "things" and made myself available to tell others of what I found to be true.

My husband and I served a mission in Ohio in 1985, and he died shortly afterwards. As a widow, I found the greatest thing I could do with my life was to tell others about this marvelous message—and especially about the Book of Mormon! I had many questions as a student of the Bible, and when I first saw the Book of Mormon I started to read it. I was absolutely astounded, and worried that I would not live long enough to benefit by its message! Since then I've served a mission in Stockholm, Sweden (temple); India; and the Family History Mission in the library in Salt Lake City. That book changed my life and direction. I'm really excited now to be assigned to the "cradle of the Restoration," where I hope to tell others what I know to be true.

I wrote children's music before joining the Church. It was for Gospel Light Publishing Company—a protestant organiza-tion. They were not happy when I called them from Rangely, Colorado, and told them I had found the true Church and had been baptized! My family was most displeased with my deci-sion—but I knew it was true!

I've written five songs for the Primary—and they are in the Children's Song Book. They have had an influence on the lives of children throughout the world—and it's all because I read the Book of Mormon.

No problem for me to go on missions the rest of my life. I'm almost down to my "things" being in a handcart. I'll keep on going as long as I stay above the ground.

—Sister Jeanne P. Lawler

This sister keeps her desire to serve alive by maintaining an eternal perspective. When you feel the presence of negative, short-term desires or worries, make the choice to shift your mind to your important lifelong objectives. Consider the "things" of real worth in life, and you'll feel those negative desires depart as you become closer to the Spirit and more resolved to do good. An anonymous author once wrote, "Desire driven by the motive to bless and serve will be fueled by one's conscience and character."

In my own life I can still remember, as a little boy, my desire to be a basketball player for BYU. A little eleven-year-old boy's desire drove him to practice outside on cold wintry days in the hope of becoming a basketball player . . . and the dream came true. If all would have and maintain the desire to fulfill their important roles within the kingdom of God, not only would we find the strength to fill those much-needed roles, but we would enjoy greater blessings of happiness here and in the hereafter. The question should echo in our soul, "What do we desire?" Eventually our thoughts and desires will take us there. Will they take you to happiness?

## A Willing Attitude

Your attitude determines almost everything in your life. It controls your outlook; the old cliché about the half-full or half-empty glass still makes a point. Our feelings and thoughts about a situation often determine our actions—and the ensuing consequences, whether they be good or bad. Wisdom literature is replete with guidance on attitude and power: "Your attitude determines your altitude." "You are what you think you are." "When things get tough, the tough get going." "As a man thinketh in his heart, so is he." The list goes on and on.

Remember, a good attitude encourages self-esteem, self-worth, and self-confidence. A good attitude brings peace, and peace in turn helps sustain a good attitude. When you are at peace with your life, as it relates to your values and behavior, your attitude toward life and others is good. The big question is: What will you do on a daily basis to maintain a positive attitude about life? Thinking of others always helps your own attitude and well-being; selfishness only hurts your attitude. Focusing on the Lord, the blessings He's given you, and your desire to give back will provide you with fuel for a fabulous attitude.

A couple in the Czech Prague Mission explained how they were able to serve a mission once they replaced their doubts with a positive attitude.

> The first obstacle we had to overcome in preparing to serve as senior missionaries was a change in attitude. Can we really learn another language, leave our comfortable home and environment, and serve in a foreign land with a different lifestyle? Yes! Yes! Yes!
>
> Once that decision was made, everything else became just a matter of organizing affairs one at a time. Get the living trust established; set up financial arrangements. Keep physically, mentally and spiritually active. Reflect on the covenants of consecration made in the temple. Serving a mission as a senior couple is an opportunity to put those covenants into practice.
>
> We solicited and received encouragement from family. The Lord opened doors so that family could live in our home. This made it easy for us to pick up and go.
>
> We spent five summers doing volunteer work for the Forest Service in primitive living conditions. We knew from experience that we could adapt and live comfortably among people with different lifestyles and customs. From the time we both served as young missionaries, and after our marriage, we began planning to serve again, together this time.
>
> Make the decision to go, then put things in order, and go!
>
> —Elder Don R. and Sister Sara-Beth Mathis

## Conclusion

As a people we are told to be of good cheer. The Lord has promised to take care of us if we keep our covenants and strive to be pure in heart—moving together as a united body of Saints toward Zion. Your attitude should be based on hope in Jesus Christ. This is the hope we want to give others. And we can, as soon as we are ready and willing to serve!

# CHAPTER 3

## RECOGNIZING YOUR POTENTIAL AS A SENIOR MISSIONARY

You are a disciple of Jesus Christ. With His help you can be more powerful than you ever imagined. When you put on that name tag you are no longer little old Sister Janet or plain old Brother Clark—you are ambassadors of the Most High God. Your calling is to serve Him by proclaiming His word to His children. Elder Bruce R. McConkie has said of your commission:

> I am called of God. My authority is above that of the kings of the earth. By revelation I have been selected as a personal representative of the Lord Jesus Christ. He is my Master and He has chosen me to represent Him. To stand in His place, to say and do what He himself would say and do if He personally were ministering to the very people to whom He has sent me. My voice is His voice, and my acts are His acts; my words are His words and my doctrine is His doctrine. My commission is to do what He wants done. To say what He wants said. To be a living modern witness in word and deed of the divinity of His great and marvelous latter-day work (*How Great Is My Calling* [address delivered while serving as president of the Australian Mission, 1961–64]).

How can we believe this? How can we feel this? How can we actually do the things Elder McConkie describes? If we give ourselves to the Lord, He will provide a way (see 1 Ne. 3:7). He will make weak things become strong (see Ether 12:27). He will be beside us (see D&C 84:85–88). He will give us the words to say if we but open our mouths (see D&C 33:8–11; 100:5–6). When we trust the Lord's strength, He will make us His instruments and we can and will do His work.

President Ezra Taft Benson emphasized this dependence on the Lord and the resulting blessings when he said:

> Men and women who turn their lives over to God will discover that He can make a lot more out of their lives than they can. He can deepen their joys, expand their vision, quicken their minds, strengthen their muscles, lift their spirits, multiply their blessings, increase their opportunities, comfort their souls, raise up friends, and pour out peace. Whoever will lose his life in the service of God will find eternal life (see Matt. 10:39) ("Jesus Christ—Gifts and Expectations," *Church News,* 14 Dec.1986).

As missionaries, we must take hold upon this promise to "lose [our] lives in the service of God to find eternal life." When you understand the magnitude of your calling and of this great work, you will be an effective missionary for the Lord.

Each missionary has been called of God. Do you understand the enormity of that? You've taken upon yourself sacred covenants. You've been empowered from on high. In my eyes, you're wonderful. You are like Nephi of old—you will with unwearyingness want to be obedient. With unwearyingness you will want to be kind to your companion. With unwearyingness you'll say your prayers; you'll do every needful thing. With unwearyingness and perseverance you'll do those things you've covenanted to do (see Hel. 10:4–6). You will know that the Lord will help you to be an instrument in His hands.

This chapter will discuss the essentials of being ambassadors of Christ, including having a testimony of Christ, having the Spirit of the Lord, and learning humility and meekness.

# Having a Testimony of Christ

As missionaries we talk of Christ, we preach of Christ, we testify of Christ (see 2 Ne. 25:26). All of us who are serving the Lord in the mission field are His disciples and ambassadors. The light that we hold (see 3 Ne. 18:24) is the Lord Jesus Christ. As Elder Hans B. Ringger so eloquently explains:

> I believe that the foundation and guiding light for all our decisions is the gospel of Jesus Christ and His message to the world. The teachings of Christ must be embedded in our desire to choose the right and in our wish to find happiness. His righteous life must be reflected in our own actions. The Lord not only teaches love, He is love. He not only preached the importance of faith, repentance, baptism, and the gift of the Holy Ghost, He lived accordingly. His life reflected the gospel that He preached. There was and is total harmony between His thoughts and His actions ("Choose You This Day," *Ensign,* May 1990, 25).

Without knowing Jesus Christ and His gospel, we cannot bear testimony of His Church and kingdom. But when we do know Christ, we can hold up His light; He is the light and the life of the world (see John 8:12). And when we hold up that light, then we truly become His disciples. Holding up the light is to share the light—the good news of the gospel.

In 3 Nephi Jesus Christ tells His disciples that they are "the light of this people" (3 Ne. 12:14), and He explains that they will bless all of Heavenly Father's children. Christ had instructed the Nephites not to put their light under a bushel, but to put it "on a candlestick, and it giveth light to all that are in the house" (3 Ne. 12:15). That same instruction applies to each of us: when we possess the light of Jesus Christ, we must not put it under a bushel. That light must be held up, and then—and only then—will we be true and worthy representatives of our Savior, Jesus Christ.

President Gordon B. Hinckley observed that we represent Christ's army. When we focus and can be His representative, we have the vision to be in His army.

In this work there must be commitment. There must be devotion. We are engaged in a great eternal struggle that concerns the very souls of the sons and daughters of God. We are not losing. We are winning. We will continue to win if we will be faithful and true. We can do it. We must do it. We will do it. There is nothing the Lord has asked of us that in faith we cannot accomplish ("The War We Are Winning," *Ensign,* Nov. 1986, 44).

We are charged to be His soldiers, true and devoted to the cause of finding and helping save our brothers and sisters. Each one of us needs help. Sister Pinegar is my keeper, and she works hard to help me do what's right. I pray that each of you will seek to be shepherds like Christ, to be your brothers' and sisters' keeper; and as you work to help each other, remember to bear testimony of Christ by your example. "Inasmuch as ye have done it unto one of the least of these my brethren, ye have done it unto me" (Matt. 25:40).

We must not, in our efforts to find and save souls, be manipulative salespeople. We must be as loving and as genuine as Christ Himself was. All the knowledge and skills we learn must be magnified by the power of God, by the attributes of Christ, by the Spirit of the Lord, and by our testimonies of this great work.

## Having the Spirit of the Lord

Remember that our capability is in the strength of the Lord as we live and are directed by the Holy Spirit. The Lord wants us to succeed and He truly will help us. When we "treasure up in [our] minds continually the words of life," the Lord has promised us that we can spread His word with confidence because we have His help (D&C 84:85).

If I would pray for anything for the missionaries scattered all over the world, I would pray that the Spirit of the Lord would come upon them with such power that they would never, ever want to do anything wrong again. When we're filled with the power of the Holy Ghost, we simply cannot sin. That's why the Nephite nation, in 3 Nephi 19:9, prayed "for that which they most desired; and they desired that the Holy Ghost should be given unto them."

Why would the Nephites desire the Holy Ghost so fervently? Elder Parley P. Pratt answered this question when he described the extraordinary characteristics of this remarkable power:

> The gift of the Holy Ghost . . . quickens all the intellectual faculties, increases, enlarges, expands and purifies all the natural passions and affections; and adapts them, by the gift of wisdom, to their lawful use. . . . It inspires virtue, kindness, goodness, tenderness, gentleness, and charity. It develops beauty of person, form, and features. It tends to health, vigor, animation, and social feeling. It develops and invigorates all the faculties of the physical and intellectual man. It strengthens, invigorates, and gives tone to the nerves. In short, it is, as it were, marrow to the bone, joy to the heart, light to the eyes, music to the ears, and life to the whole being (*Key to the Science of Theology,* 101–2).

A powerful testimony coupled with the Spirit is a strong instrument of conversion. Just because you can't speak the language or know all the discussions, don't ever think your testimony isn't strong, because it is. Every testimony that's borne is not borne of man, but borne of God by the power of the Holy Ghost. When we bear testimony it's not simply you or me speaking; it's also the Spirit of God, and that's powerful.

Just the other day I got a letter from a missionary that illustrates the power of the Holy Ghost in missionary work. "Dear President Pinegar," it started, "We didn't know what we were doing. We didn't know which way was up, but we took ten copies of the Book of Mormon, we placed ten copies, and we have nine referrals. Is that pretty good?"

Pretty good? This elder confessed up front that he didn't know all the discussions. He didn't know every word to say. But he loved the Lord and loved the person he was talking to, and when he bore testimony of the Book of Mormon, that testimony went into the other person's heart—a perfect illustration of the power of the Holy Ghost "carrying" the message unto hearts, as spoken of in 2 Nephi 33:1.

## Learning Humility and Meekness

The Book of Mormon instructs us to become humble or we will not learn (see 2 Ne. 9:42). In Ether we are told that becoming humble is, in fact, an important part of the process of learning, recognizing our weaknesses, and becoming strong and great in the Lord's hands. "And if men come unto me I will show unto them their weakness. I give unto men weakness that they may be humble; and my grace is sufficient for all men that humble themselves before me; for if they humble themselves before me, and have faith in me, then will I make weak things become strong unto them" (Ether 12:27). Meekness is also spoken of several times in connection with humility. "Blessed are the meek; for they shall inherit the earth" (Matt. 5:5). If we are easily entreated, eager to be taught, and anxious in our pursuit of becoming like Christ, *even as He is*, we may be considered meek (3 Ne. 27:27).

Certainly the people in the Book of Mormon had a hard time with humility, and truth be told, we have a hard time too. But we are told that when God loves a people, He chastens them (see Heb. 12:6). Chastening often results in humility, and we cannot carry out the will of the Lord without being humble enough to follow it. Several dictionaries define *meekness* as a willingness to suffer patiently without resentment—to give room for chastening to teach us. Meekness is that quality of willingness to listen, to change, and to grow. Meekness is a fruit of humility.

Elder Richard G. Scott describes the virtues of humility and meekness, detailing the glorious gifts that result when we apply them in our lives.

> Humility is the precious, fertile soil of righteous character. It germinates the seeds of personal growth. When cultivated through the exercise of faith, pruned by repentance, and fortified by obedience and good works, such seeds produce the cherished fruit of spirituality (see Alma 26:22) ("The Plan for Happiness and Exaltation," *Ensign,* Nov. 1981, 11).

He then explains that this spirituality includes divine inspiration and power—inspiration to "know the will of the Lord" and power to "accomplish that inspired will."

Humility and meekness are the beginning virtues of all spiritual growth. Until we have them, we cannot grow. You recall when Alma was teaching the Zoramites; many were humbled because they were cast out of the synagogue. And it was those who were cast out of the synagogue who listened to Alma and his message (see Alma 31–32). The wealthy and haughty Zoramites, those climbing up on the Rameumptom and praying, did not hear the word of God or feel the Spirit of the Lord. Humility is indeed the key to hearing and obeying the word of God.

Humble missionaries recognize the truth of President Lorenzo Snow's observation: "The Lord has not chosen the great and learned of the world to perform His work on the earth . . . but humble men [and women] devoted to His cause . . . who are willing to be led and guided by the Holy Spirit and who will of necessity give the glory unto Him, knowing that of themselves they can do nothing" (*Teachings of Lorenzo Snow*, 77). Being humble involves trusting the Lord and giving all glory to Him. But we can do it, for the Lord will be with us.

Humility and meekness also lead to righteousness and goodness. That's why I just love to be around senior missionaries, teaching them, because they are so willing to accept the teachings of the Lord. I tingle when I think what a great honor and joy it is to teach the senior missionaries at the MTC; their righteous willingness is inspiring and touching.

Humility is a state of mind and being. It is recognizing our relationship and dependence upon our Heavenly Father. Our prayers should reflect our humility: "Our Father in Heaven . . . We ask Thee." In this humble and meek state we are magnified by the Lord. We can do the things He would have us do. As we pray, our humility becomes stronger and stronger (see Hel. 3:35) and our power to do good is fortified by the infinite power of God. We become totally independent of the world when we are dependent upon our God.

I think of the couples I served with in the England London South Mission. They baptized at almost the same rate as the younger missionaries and still did all the activation and retention work. Couples in our mission would go out some days and knock on doors and simply trust in the Lord . . . and yes, they had success. They would find investigators who would listen and even find some old members who had gone astray. They were so good. I sometimes just stop and think of their goodness and my eyes well up with tears. Now every week I teach at the Senior MTC and see these humble, devoted disciples of the Lord and my heart leaps with joy. The senior missionaries are truly Saints of the most high God devoted to serving their God and their fellowmen.

How is it possible to have the success of these couples in England? Simple: it happened because of the humility of these devoted missionaries. They gave themselves to the Lord and asked every day, "Father, what would thou have us do?" And then they went out and did it.

No matter how great we are, we can always improve. None of us are perfect. But we must be humble enough to serve, and submit to the will of the Lord—giving Him the gift of our hearts. Whenever the people in the Book of Mormon were prideful or disobedient, the Lord humbled them so they could grow. Even when the people were doing well, the Lord sent prophets to exhort them to continually improve. Sometimes they sank back into wickedness and the Lord still exhorted them. Sometimes this brought about change, and sometimes it didn't. Our quest should be to always be humble enough to change.

In the Book of Mormon we read that humility can bring about a great change of heart and ultimately, salvation. Alma observes at one point during his teaching, "And behold, [Alma the Elder] preached the word unto your fathers, and a mighty change was also wrought in their hearts, and they humbled themselves and put their trust in the true and living God. And behold, they were faithful until the end; therefore they were saved" (Alma 5:13). Notice how it is humility, being meek and lowly, that creates a place for the word in our hearts, and the word then brings a willingness to change—and that change brings power.

## Conclusion

We must honestly look at ourselves and evaluate our lives and actions. Each day we can say, "I am a divine child of God, and I can be better each day, a step at a time." Don't overwhelm yourself; but whether you're nineteen or ninety-nine, each day strive to be better than you were the day before. Hold up the light of your testimony, pray for the power of the Holy Ghost in your teaching, and be humble enough to take counsel from the Lord.

The Lord is so good to us. Elder Neal A. Maxwell reminds us if we are but willing and available the Lord can do the rest. "God does not begin by asking us about our ability, but only about our avail-ability, and if we then prove our dependability, he will increase our capability!" ("It's Service, Not Status, That Counts," *Ensign,* July 1975, 7).

Oh, you senior missionaries are so good! Your testimony will grow because you'll have a vision of who you are. You will have the Holy Ghost and therefore possess the pure love of Christ that He has for His children. You'll choose to be humble and obedient because you love your God.

Each day I pray that you'll take a moment to look in the mirror (maybe the mirror could even have a picture of Christ taped to it) and evaluate your life according to what we've just discussed. Then go and do as Jesus would do. Every day let us be as the Savior would have us be. And what manner of men and women ought we to be? The Savior tells us: "Therefore I would that ye should be perfect even as I, or your Father who is in heaven is perfect" (3 Ne. 12:48).

Your capacity is limitless and your potential is like unto angels of God. As senior missionaries you have had a lifetime of preparation to serve the Lord as full-time missionaries. You are devoted disciples already having proved yourselves in Church service all your life. You can represent the Lord as His ambassadors in a variety of missionary service opportunities. You are His divine children with a wonderful opportunity to fulfill the measure of your creation—to build up the kingdom of God by blessing others and bringing souls to Christ. And you can do it with the testimony, talents, and skills you presently have. Remember Elder Maxwell's words:

The large attributes, those that cover the most ground, are almost always developed incrementally—by small steps, small decisions, and small initiatives. These attributes and talents we bring with us from the premortal world were most likely developed there in the same way. Yet upon seeing someone with highly developed cardinal attributes, we may respond that "he was born that way." Whatever the case, so far as the mortal life is concerned, it is what we do with these qualities that matters (Neal A. Maxwell, *If Thou Endure It Well,* 35).

Take the qualities you have and follow Elder Maxwell's advice to bring souls unto Christ. I love you; I honor you. I thank God that you are here to carry the gospel to His children upon the earth. May God bless you in your endeavors to do so.

# CHAPTER 4

## OVERCOMING CONCERNS OF HOME

Our devotion and dedication to building up the kingdom of God is overshadowed by the Lord's goodness and His willingness to bless us. The Lord will take care of our homes and families (in ways we can't begin to imagine) as we take care of the rest of His family in the mission field.

Peter, the great Apostle of the Lord, worriedly talked of having left all and followed Christ. The Lord reminds Peter that he will receive blessings of a hundredfold, indicating that he's not really giving anything up by the sacrifice. That in fact he will receive more than he sacrificed, including blessings regarding his family and temporal welfare, on top of the ultimate blessing of eternal life (see JST, Mark 10:27–30).

## Obedience = Blessings

The eternal law of the harvest is continually evident before us as seeds are planted and the harvest of the fruit comes forth. This law is scripturally explained as follows: "There is a law, irrevocably decreed in heaven before the foundations of this world, upon which all blessings are predicated—And when we obtain any blessing from God, it is by obedience to that law upon which it is predicated" (D&C 130: 20–21).

Obedience is the first law of heaven, and every observance of the law brings forth blessings. It may be hard to obey at times, but the Lord will make it worthwhile. Will there be days when trials and tribulations come upon us? Of course. But we must face those trials, doubts, and fears with faith as the stripling warriors did: "We cannot doubt," (see Alma 56:48) they said; "Our mothers taught us" (see Alma 57:21). And neither can we, for the Lord Jesus Christ has taught us that our obedience will warrant blessings of an hundred-fold. He also said, "I, the Lord, am bound when ye do what I say; but when ye do not what I say, ye have no promise" (D&C 82:10).

From these two scriptures we learn an eternal verity: our Heavenly Father will bless His children. He wants to shower down blessings to His children. The principle is simple—the law of the harvest: as ye sow so shall ye reap. As you progress in obedience to commandments, you will be blessed accordingly in this life and the next. The blessings associated with sacrifice, missionary work, and enduring to the end are magnificent for you as an individual and for your family, from forgiveness of sins (see D&C 31:5) to eternal life (see 2 Ne. 33:4).

## Leaving Home and Hearth in the Lord's Hands

The Lord is our shepherd. He has infinite concern for both our spiritual and temporal happiness. When we realize this, our trust in the Lord and confidence will wax strong and we will know that our families and homes are well, even as the Lord promised the Prophet Joseph and Sidney Rigdon when he asked them to leave their families and go on missions.

> Verily, thus saith the Lord unto you, my friends Sidney and Joseph, your families are well; they are in mine hands, and I will do with them as seemeth me good; for in me there is all power.
>
> Therefore, follow me, and listen to the counsel which I shall give unto you (D&C 100:1–2).

Elder Hales reminds us of the Lord's promise to Thomas B. Marsh, who was greatly worried about leaving his family in order to fulfill his mission:

In 1830 the Lord called Thomas B. Marsh to leave his family and go into the mission field. Brother Marsh was greatly concerned about leaving his family at that time. In a tender revelation, the Lord told him, "I will bless you and your family, yea, your little ones. . . . Lift up your heart and rejoice, for the hour of your mission is come. . . . Wherefore, your family shall live. . . . Go from them only for a little time, and declare my word, and I will prepare a place for them" (D&C 31:2–3, 5–6) (*Ensign*, May 2001, 26).

One sister testifies of how the Lord's promise to the early missionaries still applies today:

Being an adult convert to the Church, I did not have the opportunity to serve a full-time mission for the Lord as a youth. I had the desire to serve and made a commitment to do so as a senior adult.

Circumstances did not look favorable at the time my husband and I retired. We had an unmarried daughter who was expecting a child, and a son serving a mission. We put our mission desires aside until our son returned from his service.

We again went to the Lord with our desires. I was personally told that all would be well. We had our interviews, submitted our papers, and waited for our call. It finally came and the old concerns surfaced again: Would our daughter and granddaughter be all right without us? I again petitioned the Lord and was told, "Do you think I would forsake you?" Here we are two years after our retirement.

—Sister N.

It is clear that the Lord did not mean those promises to apply only to Joseph, Sidney, and Thomas B. Marsh, but that he made such specific promises to every missionary who seeks to put the Lord first. In Doctrine and Covenants 118:3 we read:

Let the residue continue to preach from that hour, and if they will do this in all lowliness of heart, in meekness and humility, and long-suffering, I, the Lord, give unto them a promise that I will provide for their families; and an effectual door shall be opened for them, from henceforth.

This same promise for temporal and spiritual blessings is echoed in Doctrine and Covenants 136:11 as well. "And if ye do this with a pure heart, in all faithfulness, ye shall be blessed; you shall be blessed in your flocks, and in your herds, and in your fields, and in your houses, and in your families."

Sister Thorup shared her feelings and described how her family was blessed:

> Our desire to serve a mission was from the fact that we have been given so much we feel we need to give some back. The blessings that have come to us in our family just since we have had our call have been breathtaking. A granddaughter who is 24 [and] needed knee surgery has recovered so fast from both knees before we left. A dear friend had back surgery and is better than she has been for years. Another granddaughter who has had a struggle in a marriage and sad relationships has just found a wonderful returned missionary and made plans to marry in the temple this August, so her small son will have a home. All this before we left.

> Go on a mission and [you learn] how much people love you. That was very humbling. This being our second mission, we realize how much our families are blessed. Two other grandchildren are changing their attitude about themselves and are much more positive. It's also a blessing to be able to go together on a mission when we have our companion still with us.

> We did much study to prepare for our farewell talks and our testimonies grew and we gained knowledge and everyone loved our talks and some wanted copies. That really is something.

> We are so thrilled and happy and feel so privileged. Our family is so supportive. We are getting great-grandchildren and a new grandson-in-law. We are blessed every day and feel the Lord is pouring on blessings.

Oh, and I forgot, my adopted (by consent) brother-in-law just got a job after five years and many of our prayers, all before we left.

—Sister Jeanne B. Thorup

Another couple describes their worries over leaving their home, and how they overcame that worry with faith, and then watched how easily everything "just worked out."

To leave on a mission [we] just had to "Do it!" [We] worked very hard for over a month to get the house and cars ready (for us to neglect them), and [then turned] the rest over to our younger sons to carry on for us. The two youngest will visit their sister (and our home) every three weeks (alternating) so that each of them is by [to check on the place] every six weeks. When they found out what we were doing, our neighbors (member or not!) volunteered to help Amy (our daughter) and Gabriella (our granddaughter) with any problem that comes up. There is no question—we are going on a mission!

—Senior Couple, MTC, 2001

Yet another couple relates their experiences with personal sickness and family duties they were concerned about. They heeded the call to serve and saw the doors of opportunity open before their eyes.

My husband and I served a mission in Russia Moscow South Mission in 1997–1998. This first time was never a question as to the concerns that normally plague seniors. We knew we wanted to serve a mission and never questioned that the Lord would take care of our family and home. He did.

After serving once, we had a great desire to serve again. My husband's parents live next to us, therefore the rest of his siblings assumed it was our responsibility to care for Mom and Dad. During our first mission our daughter lived in our home. She cared for Mom and Dad (Grandma and Grandpa) as well. As we contemplated a second mission, we knew and felt that we could not impose this responsibility on her again. [Our] parents were aged and [required] a great deal of care. Father [was] 93 and totally dependant, not being able to walk, hear, see, etc. Most days he knew no one. Mother [was] 88, partly blind, but still able to take care of their simple needs. We kept their yard, cooked for them, and did all necessities—shopping, etc. This went on for three years. We were kept every day caring for their needs.

Just before the conference in April 2001, when the great call for senior missionaries was issued, my husband's sister announced she and her husband were selling their house. They would move in with Mom and Dad!!! We were elated. That very Sunday we picked up our papers from the bishop. We felt a strong urgency to be quick about filling them out and turning them in.

Our call came. We had one month to make all arrangements and be in Singapore. Our home! What to do? We prayed about it. Within two days we had a call from a single gal wanting to house-sit for us. We told her we would pray about it. The answer came, "All the earth is mine." We share what we have with our sister. That was settled. Then my husband and I began to be plagued with physical ailments, none we'd ever had before. I would (kiddingly) say to my husband, "The devil has me." We were so determined to serve again that no amount of adversity would hold us back and our ailments fled.

The week before we left for our mission, our daughter who had a civil marriage was sealed to her husband and children. Our son's wife, who has been unable to have a child became pregnant. We feel confident that there will be a new grandchild when we return. Our grandchildren, how we love them. As I write, tears come!! Our faith is such that we know all will be well.

—Elder and Sister Hansen

Finally, this sister's testimony sums up how the Lord not only takes care of our homes and families, but that He assures us that He has—so we don't worry.

I am very happy that I decided to come on this mission. My concern was that I was not able to find someone to take care of my many little responsibilities that I have at home. But once I made up my mind, the Spirit touched me so, and I felt so good about my decision. I was blessed in so many ways. Everything I needed to do fell into place remarkably well. It is a joy how the Lord has strengthened me. I want to serve and be His hands here on the earth to bring people back into his fold. I have a deep testimony of the gospel that it is true, and I will find many people in West Virginia to share my feelings with.

—Sister Christel Sanford

## Leaving a Legacy of Righteousness

Benjamin Franklin once said, "A good example is the best sermon" (*Poor Richard's Almanach,* 74). The power of example leaves a legacy in the lives of the people we love and can influence. Example is a powerful teacher. It is a model or pattern for living. As the old adage makes clear, actions speak louder than words—the power of example is often greater than that of our carefully prepared lessons of words. We all follow examples from the day we're born to the day we die. Just as when we mimicked our parents as little children, and as we grew into adulthood carting the tendencies learned in the home, we too are now examples to others—for good or for ill—every moment of our lives and even after we're gone. Elder Hales of the Quorum of the Twelve has said:

> If we are willing to leave our loved ones for service in the mission field, we will bless them with a heritage that will teach and inspire them for generations to come.
>
> It is significant to me that after commanding the Brethren to teach their children light and truth and set their families in order, the Lord immediately called them on missions. "Now, I say unto you, my friends, let my servant Sidney Rigdon go on his journey, and make haste, and also proclaim . . . the gospel of salvation" (D&C 93:51) (*Ensign,* May 2001, 25).

The Lord recognized that a crucial part of the Brethren's being able to teach their children light and truth in such hard times (imagine how that applies now!) was by being an example. We cannot choose *not* to be an example, but we can choose to be a good one. It is a matter of choice. Think of your life as a garden of love. Through your example, you are planting good seeds for the coming generation. What you cultivate in your garden will grow into plants that will bear good fruit and nourish the lives of others.

Point out to your family the good examples of forebearers so that your children will be rooted in the principles that endure. Elder Hales applied this truth to missionary work:

> As we serve in the mission field, our children and grandchildren will be blessed in ways that would not have been possible had we stayed at home. Talk to couples who have served missions and they will tell you of blessings poured out: inactive children activated, family members baptized, and testimonies strengthened because of their service. . . .
>
> The Lord will send special blessings to your family as you serve. "I, the Lord, give unto them a promise that I will provide for their families" (D&C 118:3). Couples are sometimes concerned that in their absence they will miss weddings, births, family reunions, and other family events. We have learned that the impact on families while grandparents are on missions is worth a thousand sermons. Families are greatly strengthened as they pray for their parents and grandparents and read letters sent home which share their testimonies and the contribution they are making in the mission field. . . .
>
> My own father and mother served a mission in England. As I visited them one day in their small flat, I watched my mother, with a shawl wrapped snugly around her shoulders, putting shillings in the gas meter to keep warm. I asked, "Why did you come on a mission, Mother?" Mother said simply, "Because I have eleven grandsons. I want them to know that Grandma and Grandpa served" (*Ensign,* May 2001, 25–26).

Another couple expressed how their mission increased their own testimonies and desire to serve—providing what they feel confident is an ongoing example for their family:

> We were blessed to serve our first mission in the "City of Joseph." The spirit that we felt there has never left our hearts and minds. We and our family were blessed with a strengthening and renewing of our testimonies. Our grandchildren have seen and felt the missionary cause. I know it will increase their own desire to serve. We are already planning our third [for] when we get back from this one.
>
> —Elder and Sister Solum

What better way to encourage our families to learn sacrifice and the vision of the work of God than to *show* them that we believe in it wholeheartedly. Albert Schweitzer summed the whole point up: "There are only three ways to teach a child. The first is by example. The second is by example. The third is by example" (quoted in *Especially for Mormons,* 82).

Another couple shared their testimony of this principle in their own lives—as they followed the example to serve.

> This is our first full-time mission and we are so thrilled to finally be here at the Senior MTC. Our parents both served missions and set the example for us. My parents' first mission was 38 years ago, and the letters they sent inspired us to set a goal to go on a mission as soon as we could retire. I retired two months ago and our papers were already in. We are thankful to serve our Heavenly Father and Savior, and pray we are useful endlessly.
>
> —Elder Harlow and Sister Peggy Brimhall

## Conclusion

Surely we will be blessed as we put our lives and the lives of our families in the hands of the Lord. Even as Christ put His life in the hands of the Father, we can be saviors on Mount Zion as we put our lives in the hands of our Lord. The indescribable joy of being a missionary for the Lord will echo in your soul, and the memory of the work will be a fountain of living water in your life.

# CHAPTER 5

## DECIDING HOW TO SERVE:
## OPTIONS AND OPPORTUNITIES

The options and opportunities for service are almost limitless. Each week bishops and stake presidents receive lists of possibilities for full-time missionary work and also for Church-service opportunities. Let your bishop know of your willingness and availability to serve in these areas. Opportunities and guidelines for missionary work will be listed in this chapter, as well as a few of the most common questions regarding costs of a mission, tax deductions, and insurance. If you have any specific questions regarding any of the following material, just check with your bishop.

## Opportunities for Full-time Missionary Service

We must remember that we are called by the Lord through His prophets. The call is extended by the prophet. You can give input and express feelings through your stake president, but your desire should be to go where the Lord needs you. If there are extenuating circumstances, those matters are always considered in the call—especially those concerning your physical well-being and medical concerns.

The following is a list of full-time missionary service areas.

- Church Education System—seminary and institute coordinators, supervisors and teachers, including BYU–Hawaii
- Facilities management—maintenance of Church sites

- Family history—variety of needs in Salt Lake City and other areas
- Farm management throughout the world
- Full-time proselyting missions (work with leadership, new converts, those that are less active, mission offices, etc.)
- Leadership and member work throughout the world
- Material management throughout the world
- Medical personnel throughout the world
- Polynesian Cultural Center
- Public affairs throughout the world
- Temple construction throughout the world
- Temple ordinance workers throughout the world
- Visitor centers throughout the world
- Welfare/humanitarian service throughout the world

### Guidelines for Full-Time Missionary Service

Full-time senior missionary opportunities usually follow these guidelines:

1. Those who serve full-time usually live away from home.
2. They must provide their own medical insurance.
3. The Church provides travel expenses to and from the field of labor.
4. Interviews are conducted by the bishop and stake president.
5. The call is extended from the prophet and the stake president will set the couple apart.
6. In the United States, the length of service is 12, 18 or 24 months. In the international areas, the length of service is 18–24 months. Couples may extend up to 30 months.
7. There are some exceptions for 6-month missions to certain visitor centers that operate for a 6-month period.

8. There is also an exception for 6-month calls that are accepted by those who are in seasonal employment, such as agriculture.

## Church-service Missions

You may want to consider a part-time Church-service mission. In most instances, Church-service missions allow you to live in your own home. You'll live on your retirement; a Church-service mission won't significantly increase expenses. Church-service missions are a wonderful way to serve when there are health problems, time restrictions, or family responsibilities that prevent you from serving full-time.

The following is a list of Church-service positions available for senior missionaries.

- Accounting and auditing
- Artist, typesetter
- Assistant in family history centers
- Assistant to the hearing impaired
- Assistant in the institute programs
- Clerical
- Computer support
- Costume shop assistant
- Driver (variety of duties)
- Editor/proofreader
- Employment assistant
- Facilities management
- Family history consultant
- Garden aide
- Host and hostess
- Inventory equipment
- Member locating

- Music typesetting
- Office worker
- Receptionist
- Sales clerk
- Secretarial transcriber
- Sign designer
- Social service assistant (substance abuse, correctional services)
- Teaching, supervising teachers
- Temple square (variety of duties)
- Tour director
- Tutor
- Visit patients in State Hospital
- Word processing

## Guidelines for Church-Service Missions

Church-service missionary opportunities usually follow these guidelines:

1. Be available to serve 4–31 hours per week. You will usually be able to live in your own home.
2. Provide your own medical expenses.
3. Travel is at your own expense.
4. Interviews are conducted by the bishop and stake president using the Church Service Recommendation form.
5. Your call will be extended by the stake president and your bishop will set you apart.
6. You can serve 6, 12, 18, or 24 months and can extend to up to 30 months if desired.

You can also volunteer to perform service for the various Church departments. This is above and beyond your ward or stake calling.

You simply tell your bishop or stake president that you are interested in serving in these ways; all such callings are considered Church-service missions.

There is a joy and a sense of honor knowing that you are doing the will of God. Parents express this joy when they know their children walk in truth (see 3 John 1:4) because of their example. Children are just the same. Their excitement is apparent when they come and tell me, "Brother Ed, my mom and dad are going to serve a mission! I'm so happy for them. They will be the greatest missionaries." A senior missionary who served in the Illinois Chicago North Mission wrote:

> Following the afternoon session of general conference (April 2001) I received a phone call from our daughter in Salt Lake. She said, "Mom, how does it feel to be right on track?"
>
> I said, "Sharon, it feels good. It feels really, really good." It does feel good, real good, to be on track. Our other children also expressed how they felt about us going on a mission at this time when so much was said about it in conference. Then later in the week, we received a letter from our youngest child who is at the MTC preparing for her mission to Portugal. She commented on the conference, then said how proud she was of us. It feels really good when your children tell you they are proud of you.
>
> We have planned to go on a mission for years and have always talked about it. It's something our children knew someday we would do. When Gary retired he was ready to go, but we have a large family and the youngest was too young. When she decided to go on a mission, then I said, "Now it's time. We can go while she is gone."
>
> I am excited about this call. When we sent in our papers, the stake president asked what type [of call we wanted] and where would we like to serve, and he wrote that down, adding we would be willing to serve wherever needed. I talked to my Heavenly Father and told Him places I thought it would be great to serve, even told Him why, but told Him I would be willing to go where He wanted me. So we are serving where He wants us. And may I add, willingly and with much joy. I feel this is where

the Lord wants us. I was never disappointed and [was] also excited. My greatest fear is [of] my own capabilities. I don't want to disappoint my Father in Heaven. I know if I put my faith and trust in the Lord I'll be okay.

The MTC has been a good experience so far. I have felt the Spirit. The instructors have been great and I'm more excited than ever to teach the gospel. Maybe I can overcome my fears and learn to put my faith in Christ after all. It is my great desire to serve Him and do His will.

—Sister Leah Jespersen

## Some Questions Often Asked

*What Is the Average Cost of a Mission?*

The cost of a mission for senior couples depends on where you serve. Most missions are between $1000 and $2000 per month—these costs are based on the standard of living in the area you serve in. Senior couples pay all their own expenses, though some missions provide a car; you can stipulate how much you can afford. You can give money to the missionary fund now even though you cannot serve. Everyone can help in their own way. The following account describes one woman's financial sacrifices and the blessings of missionary service that soon followed.

I began earnestly planning possibilities of serving a mission by "pinching pennies" to a substantial sum and by selling my car. Some of our concerns were money, which I had saved; our home, which a daughter wanted; and my husband's truck, which a neighbor purchased.

We were blessed with an "impossible dream" coming true by being called to serve in the choice land of Tonga, where we are really enjoying the wonderful, faithful, friendly Tongans. We enjoy their strong spirit, their beautiful temple, and their singing.

—Sister G. Emma Bowker

*Are Mission Costs Tax Deductible?*

In a letter from the Presiding Bishopric on the 23 December 1992, priesthood leaders were told that "couples living away from home and with duplicate housing costs may, in some instances, deduct costs for housing, food, etc." However, they advised consulting a tax adviser before making such deductions. Senior missionaries were also instructed not to channel their funds through their bishops, but to pay mission costs directly in the field.

*What About Health Insurance?*

Couples serving full-time or Church-service missions must have medical or health insurance. There are policies available for those interested. Couples serving in the United States should keep their Medicare, and those going out of the country are encouraged to keep their own retirement insurance where applicable.

Elder David B. Haight has outlined information that's helpful to know when receiving a call to serve as senior couples. He also indicates that health factors will be taken into consideration when this call is issued:

> All missionary calls come from the Lord through inspiration to His servants. Therefore, it is not appropriate for couples to dictate where they will serve. President Howard W. Hunter said, "When we know why we serve, it won't matter where we serve!" However, we want to know as much as possible about potential couple missionaries, including what type of assignment they might like.
>
> When couple missionaries and sister missionaries apply to serve a mission, they fill out an additional form that provides us with such information as past employment experience, education or training, language skills, Church positions, special skills, abilities, interests, hobbies, and limitations or special circumstances. This information is considered when making assignments, as are age and health. Even couples who respond to openings listed in the "Church Service Missionary Opportunities" bulletin may express their interest in a particular assignment, but the final decision still rests with the Brethren (*Ensign,* Feb. 1996, 9).

## Conclusion

The possibilities for service are many and varied. And service in the Lord's kingdom is the best work we will ever do. This senior couple outlines the surprising ease of serving if we put our faith in the Lord.

> If you really want to go on a mission, it is possible. The Church makes allowances for older people. Your workload is easier than the young missionaries. Your health and age are taken into consideration.
>
> Find someone reliable to take care of your home and yard while you are away. Above all, don't worry about it. The Lord will bless you for all that you do, and this includes your health and your possessions.
>
> You can arrange with a doctor and druggist to send your medicine to you. It is surprising how much you can stretch your money when you are on your mission. Somehow your necessities aren't all that expensive.
>
> Think of all the wonderful experiences you will be having, the joy of explaining the gospel to others, the joy of baptizing and blessing others. Think of the example you are setting for your children and grandchildren. Think of all the struggling branches and little wards in faraway places that you can help with your knowledge of the gospel, and priesthood support you can give. Oh, how the world needs you blessed older people with your white hair making halos around your heads!
>
> —Sister Jean and Elder Richard Taylor

The opportunities and options are here. We simply need to make ourselves available. The Lord does not require us to run faster than we have strength. He, through His prophet, has given us a great many choices—length of service, when we serve, types of service, etc. We just need to say yes, and then the joy is ours just like Alma described (see Alma 29:9–10).

# CHAPTER 6

## CONQUERING YOUR FEARS

Fear is one of the greatest deterrents to action—it is one of Satan's most valuable tools. Elder Robert D. Hales has taught us how to abolish fear so we can build up the kingdom of God.

> Fear of the unknown or fear that we don't have the scriptural skills or language required can cause reluctance to serve. But the Lord has said, "If ye are prepared ye shall not fear" (D&C 38:30). Your life is your preparation. You have valuable experience. You have raised a family and served in the Church. Just go and be yourselves. The Lord has promised that angels will go before you (see D&C 103:19–20). You will be told by the Spirit what to say and when to say it in a very natural process as you strengthen young missionaries, testify to investigators and new members, teach leadership skills, and friendship and fellowship less-active members, helping them return to full activity. *You* are the testimony, and you will touch the lives of those with whom you come in contact. Couples normally do not tract and are not expected to memorize discussions or maintain the same schedule as young elders and sisters. Simply be yourself. Serve to the best of your ability, and the Lord will bless you (*Ensign,* May 2001, 25, italics in the original).

Elder Hales has said it all: the Lord will qualify us and keep us safely beyond the shackles of fear if we trust in His promises.

## Overcoming Fears

Sometimes as missionaries we are afraid to do our duty. We just can't do it. Fear and doubt have overcome us. In my experience, missionaries who had the hardest time in the mission field were the ones who were afraid, who were filled with doubt, and who thought they couldn't do it. So we have to learn how to overcome fear. Fear and doubt can be overcome with five things: faith, love, knowledge, preparation, and experience.

### Faith

If you exercise faith and mentally exert the power that accompanies it, fear and doubt will flee away. One brother, Elder Elvin C. Hall, tells how simple the choice to have faith is; "How did I become a senior missionary? It happened much the same way as when I went on my first mission in the 1950s. I just assumed I would when the time came. Though I had fears and uncertainties, I trust in the Lord's support when I commit to do His work."

The Apostles of old asked the Savior to increase their faith (see Luke 17:5); we should do the same, but we should also take action to help the Lord help us. Faith comes by hearing the word of the Lord. Every time you read the scriptures, every time you hear your president speak, every time you talk together as companions, the word of the Lord will come into your heart and your faith will increase, and you will become like Nephi and Lehi, the sons of Helaman, whose faith was so strong that they converted thousands of people (see Ether 12:14). Mighty prayer destroys doubt and fear—thus increasing faith. "They did fast and pray oft, and did wax stronger and stronger in their humility, and firmer and firmer in [their] faith" (Hel. 3:35). Faith is the first step toward decreasing your fear.

We must bolster our choice to have faith by studying the Lord's promises and incorporating those truths into our lives. A senior sister records her experiences in learning to have faith based on the promises in the scriptures.

> As a single, senior missionary, I was sitting on my bed in our little apartment when thoughts of home and family came

unbidden, and a great longing for loved ones far away swept over me. Letters from home came often, bringing happy reports of grandchildren, several who did not even remember me; some contained mention of activities and concerns of young parents; and some carried guarded messages of my parents struggling with the problems of aging. A feeling of great loneliness and sadness crept into my heart.

I don't remember how the Spirit directed my study that morning, but I was drawn to the scripture in Luke and the words seemed to speak directly to me from heaven in answer to my longing. [Luke 18:29–30, which reads, "There is no man that hath left house, or parents, or brethren, or wife, or children, for the kingdom of God's sake, Who shall not receive manifold more in this present time, and in the world to come life everlasting."] My heart was comforted and renewed again in the knowledge of the importance of the work that I was called to do in the mission field. I knew that heaven was aware of me and my feelings, and the Lord was including me in the promise of blessings "in this present time, and in the world to come life everlasting."

With the peace of that assurance, I knelt and thanked a kind Heavenly Father for His love and the guidance of the scriptures. I am grateful for the opportunity to be a missionary, offering that same peace and guidance, and many more blessings, to all who will listen and accept His gospel ("Living by the Scriptures," *Church News,* 9 Nov. 1996).

There is nothing too hard for you and the Lord to overcome. The following scripture should give us the hope that will increase our faith to trust in the Lord. Ponder it and you shall receive courage to do the will of God. "Trust in the Lord with all thine heart; and lean not unto thine own understanding. In all thy ways acknowledge him, and he shall direct thy paths" (Prov. 3:5–6).

The prophets of old have demonstrated the principle of trust from Adam to Moses, from Father Lehi to Moroni, and in our day from the Prophet Joseph to the prophet Gordon B. Hinckley. As we witness the works of these great Brethren, we often think, *Well, they're the prophets. They're so much better than I am.* Remember that the

Brethren are subject to all the same anxieties of mortality that we are, but they have overcome. Many of them have recorded saying, "Not me . . . surely not me. I'm slow of speech . . ." and the reasons go on. But they trust in God and are validated in life. This is exactly what our Savior Jesus Christ did. He trusted in the Father to direct His mission to success, and when the great moment of fear came, that trust resulted in His ability to finish the Father's will.

There are examples of faith fulfilled from the pioneers back to those who boarded the ships of Nephi and the Jaredite barges. They were human just like you and me.

Senior missionaries have told me, "We just trusted in the Lord and we knew everything would be okay." Isn't that marvelous? We must adopt that attitude and act accordingly. Surely we should do as Proverbs 3:5 has taught us, to "lean not to [our] own understanding" but instead to trust in the one who sees beyond "our ways" to the true way.

Nephi recorded his decision to do so in his wonderful psalm: "O Lord, I have trusted in thee, and I will trust in thee forever. I will not put my trust in the arm of flesh; for I know that cursed is he that putteth his trust in the arm of flesh. Yea, cursed is he that putteth his trust in man or maketh flesh his arm" (2 Ne. 4:34). And Christ Himself has validated Nephi's statement: "If ye will have faith in me ye shall have power to do whatsoever thing is expedient in me" (Moro. 7:33).

There is nothing more expedient and urgent than helping Heavenly Father's children return to His presence. As senior missionaries we are only asked to love and serve others. Concerns? No, just trust in the Lord and exercise your faith and you shall be blessed, just like Elder and Sister Homer describe in the *Church News:*

> After suffering severe hearing loss, I felt my desire to serve a mission would not be realized. At home, I had such good support, family, friends, and ward family. But putting our trust in the Lord, my husband and I came on a mission.
>
> Of course, it has required us to crawl out of our comfort zone, but to have missed knowing and loving the people of South Africa would have been such a loss to us.

Serving a mission is a lot like paying tithing—you don't pay tithing with money, but with faith. So is serving a mission as a retired couple.

Another senior couple interviewed in the article said how simply the many issues of concern can be resolved—how easy the choice to go really is:

1. Have faith in the Lord; He will guide you, give you strength.
2. Realize your mission will bless your family; you are setting a positive example.
3. Put temporal affairs in order one at a time; plan ahead.
4. Realize your maturity and gospel experience is needed; expect wonderful blessings ("How to Overcome Obstacles to Serving a Mission as a Retired Couple," *Church News,* 29 March 1997).

## *Love*

Perfect love casteth out all fear (see 1 John 4:18). Think about it. If you are full of love, then there is no room for fear. When love is in your heart, how you feel about the worth of souls is overwhelming. You will have such concern that you will do anything to help them come unto Christ—you won't fear doing a single thing. Such was the example of the sons of Mosiah in their concern for their fellowmen (see Mosiah 28:3). They served fearlessly for fourteen years at the peril of their lives—just to have the chance to gather a few more souls unto Christ.

Our fears are not always as compelling as fear for our lives. We might fear facing discomfort and what lies beyond our comfort zones. We might also fear our weaknesses or inabilities, letting others—or ourselves—down, or not being able to conquer any number of personal challenges or those associated with our calling, or we simply fear that we don't have the capability to endure difficulty to the end. Mother Teresa tells two interesting stories of how love and a vision of the worth of souls erased two mothers' fears, and made what seemed insurmountable struggles into simple daily tasks—even blessings.

I remember a mother of twelve children, the last of them terribly mutilated. It is impossible for me to describe the creature. I volunteered to welcome the child into our house, where there are many others in similar conditions. The woman began to cry. "For [Heaven's] sake, Mother," she said, "don't tell me that. This [child] is the greatest gift of God to me and my family. All our love is focused on her. Our lives would be empty if you took her from us. . . ."

I will [also] never forget one day in Venezuela when I went to visit a family who had given us a lamb. I went to thank them and there I found out that they had a badly crippled child. I asked the mother, "What is the child's name?" The mother gave me a most beautiful answer.

"We call him 'Teacher of Love,' because he keeps on teaching us how to love. Everything we do for him is our love for God in action" (*Mother Teresa, No Greater Love*, 24–25).

Just as everything Christ and Heavenly Father have done is Their love for us in action, everything we do should be "our love for God in action." Just as the Savior faced the most difficult challenge in the universe out of love for us, we will find that following this pattern of action is how life's choices become simple—made with love as the motive. No fear or challenge or calamity is beyond the healing, teaching reach of love—either our challenges or those of our brothers and sisters we are trying to bring unto the God of love. Learn to love, to think of each person you meet as a "Teacher of Love," and your heart will hold no room for fear.

*Knowledge*

Knowledge is power. When you see and understand, you know what's out there and you're never afraid. I remember when I was little and afraid of the dark. I'd ask, "Can you leave the light on just a little bit?" And then I wouldn't be quite so afraid. But then one time when I was a little boy we saw a bad movie. It was something like *Frankenstein Meets the Werewolf with the Mummy*. I know that sounds funny. I mean, now it would be a G-rated movie and we'd say, "Oh look how funny it is," but in those days I was just a little nine-year-old boy, and I hid behind the seats. At the same time I saw that movie we were living on a farm. To irrigate our orchards we would receive water from Strawberry Reservoir. The times when it was our turn to receive the irrigation water were called "water turns." Well, this one time our water turn came at midnight. Now, my duty as the youngest boy, the baby of the family, was to do whatever my big brothers said. So my job was to go down to the end of the furrow, and when the water got there say, "The water's here," and that's all I had to do. But, you must understand, it's midnight and there's a full moon. You know the werewolf is going to come; he's going to be there—there's no way out of it. So I started walking down the row, and the pheasants are flying by, and I think, *Heavenly Father, I'm going to be a good boy. Don't let me die.* I was afraid. Why was I so afraid? Because I couldn't see. There was no light. I was afraid because of the past experience of that movie. When you get enough knowledge, when you see clearly, you will have power, and then fear will flee from you. That's how knowledge overpowers fear.

### Preparation

Life is full of trials and tribulations. Opposition is at every corner it seems and change is difficult. Often times we aren't prepared for change, and that makes the change scary. When I served at the MTC, I came to realize that one of the main adjustments for the missionaries was the radical change in their lifestyle: the intensity of the expected work ethic and the new challenges and fears they were asked to face. This change is hard on everyone, young and old alike. Recognizing that we must venture beyond our comfort zones will help us be prepared to overcome our fears and resolve our concerns.

When you're prepared, fear is overcome because you understand how to face a challenge—you're not just barging into the darkness without defense, because you have means with which to face what lies ahead. Preparation, like knowledge, is power. Self-confidence and self-reliance increase with your level of preparation.

When the vision and desire are in place, then preparation becomes the master. It takes time, effort, dedication, and often sacrifice in order to prepare well. Make yourself fully capable of doing all that is required. Put in the time to study and pray and exert yourself.

With this aspect of your mission in place, you will feel more in control, fear will not be part of your life, and you can expect greater success. You have already prepared well for missionary work, and you can enjoy the blessing of success as you engage in inspired missionary training.

<u>Pre-MTC Instruction</u>: A program called Pre-MTC Language Training, available only in Utah in Russian, Spanish, Portuguese, and French, has proven very effective. Senior missionaries begin studying the language at home as soon as they receive their calling. Their study is bolstered by a tutor from the Missionary Training Center who telephones twice a week to give help. Brother Barton, one of several training directors, comments on the results:

> This pre-training program really gives them a leg up. . . . New missionaries with pre-training enter at the level reached by those who have completed their training period. Their confidence level is much higher and they function better ("Seniors Train at Their Own Pace," *Church News,* 15 Aug. 1992).

<u>Senior MTC Training</u>: Your experience in the senior MTC will allay your fears and fill you with the Spirit—making you eager and ready to serve. At the Senior MTC you will review important gospel principles and doctrines, learn some principles and missionary skills that will assist you in your work—including some missionary discussions (and, remember, you already know the doctrine), family history overview, leadership pointers, and knowledge of the culture in the area you have been called to serve.

Specialized instruction is given to you in regard to your individual assignment, and your length of stay varies according to it as well, usually around a week, unless you are learning a language, then it is approximately eight to nine weeks.

*Experience*

Most concerns of senior missionaries are from *unfounded* fears brought on by difficulties in leaving our comfort zone and simply not understanding our new situation, which causes anxiety and frustration.

Like all other changes in life, once we have gone through them we feel confident functioning in our new comfort zone. We simply have to stretch and get out of our current comfort zone and trust in the Lord. The more we do a thing the more our fear decreases. When I was a mission president in the England London South Mission, the new missionaries spent their first day training in proselyting. The assistants to the president would teach them the dialogues and how to open their mouths. Then we'd send them out on the streets to meet people, just to open their mouths. The experience would go something like this: "Would you be so kind and friendly as to answer a few questions that could bless your life? It'll only take a minute." That was the big number one question, after which we had them ask questions about life, our Savior, family, the Book of Mormon, etc. But, it was just that simple, "Hi, would you be so kind and friendly as to answer a few questions?" And after one day the experience helped conquer their fear. When we recognize that we are instruments in God's hands, disciples of Jesus Christ and filled with love, we can open our mouths. (You are not even required to tract, so you've got less fear to conquer from the beginning!)

Though fear and doubt are natural feelings when we move out of our comfort zone, we should approach those two terrors with the same promises (to ourselves) we gave our children when they were fearful of going to school for the first time, "Remember, sweetheart, Heavenly Father will help you and after a few days everything will be fine . . . you'll see." As our advice echoes in our own minds, we should take courage knowing that all we're going to do is head out to the school of loving people. We'll simply be helping our "extended" family, just like we helped our friends, neighbors, and loved ones back home. We have no need to worry. There is a light at the end of the tunnel and our joy will be indescribably delicious as we move toward it.

## Open Your Mouth

If we examine Doctrine and Covenants 33:8, "Open your mouths and they shall be filled," and Doctrine and Covenants 130 again, the verse indicating that all blessings are based on laws of obedience (130:20–21), we will discover that the law that matters most on your mission is the law to open your mouth.

The Lord cautioned us against hiding behind our fear (thereby demonstrating that we do not trust Him): "But with some I am not well pleased, for they will not open their mouths, but they hide the talent which I have given unto them, because of the fear of man. Wo unto such, for mine anger is kindled against them. And it shall come to pass, if they are not more faithful unto me, it shall be taken away, even that which they have" (D&C 60:2–3). We must overcome our fears so that we can find Heavenly Father's children and preach with power. They too can then enjoy the gospel of Jesus Christ.

I'll never forget when I served as a mission president in the MTC. The last meeting before the missionaries would go out, I would speak about being bold, obedient, full of love, and courageous in opening their mouths. "Do not be afraid. The worth of souls is great. You have a mighty role in the kingdom." Well, some of them were still afraid. I would ask them on their way to their mission to have a finding experience of opening their mouths. This sweet young sister wrote me a letter after she'd been out two weeks, and this is how it went:

> Dear President, after your talk Sunday night I was so nervous I didn't know what to do. I knew I'd be leaving Wednesday, and I was going to have to open my mouth. And I thought, *I can't do it, I can't do it.* So I fasted and I prayed and I left Wednesday on the plane, and to my joy I had a window seat and my companion sat next to me. So I said, "Oh dear I won't be able to talk to anybody on the plane," and so I was relieved.
>
> But then, I got into the airport and I sat down, and here was a man sitting across from me. He was old and different looking, and I didn't know what to do. And all I could remember was your voice telling us, "Open your mouths, it will be filled, I promise you." Well, I girded up my loins and I opened my mouth and said, "Hi, where you headed?" From that little beginning began an hour conversation. Pretty soon we became friends. And after a bit I said, "If you knew there was another book written about Jesus Christ would you be interested in reading that? The Book of Mormon?"
>
> He said, "Oh, I have a Book of Mormon." I committed him right there to read the book, and then he told me, "My daughter is taking the discussions too."

And then I said, "Is it okay if I have the missionaries come by and see you?"

He said, "That will just be fine." Oh, President, it's so easy to open your mouth. The Lord will fill it. There's nothing to it. Tell all the missionaries, young and old alike, *they can do it.*

I read that letter every time to departing missionaries because it helped them realize that we can all do it. All of us, member missionary and full-time proselyting missionaries, can open our mouths and they will be filled.

When we open our mouths, sometimes we don't know exactly what to say. So in our mission there was a rule: you could not pass anyone on the street without saying, "Excuse me, would you be so kind and friendly as to answer a few questions?" And pretty soon, all the missionaries understood, and all of a sudden baptisms weren't thirty a month, but they were a hundred and thirty a month. Why? Because the Lord blessed the missionaries because they were obedient and had faith in His promises.

Here is one of the most beautiful parts of the process. If you've studied, if you've pleaded with the Lord, and if you're worthy and desire righteousness—you're being obedient—then words and ideas will come out of your mouth that you've never even known.

The other day I was speaking to a group, and afterwards a man came up to me and said, "That was the most profound statement I've ever heard in my life."

"What was?" I asked.

"When you said that truth without testimony is hollow." He had it written down on a piece of paper.

"Wow," I said. "Who said that?"

"You did."

"When?" I asked.

"Just now, in that room."

"Can I write that down?" So I wrote it down, and now I'm sharing it with you. And why was I able to say that? Because the Lord inspires us; sometimes we don't even realize what we've said! President Marion G. Romney once observed that he always knew when he had spoken by the Spirit because he learned from what he had said (Don J. Black, *A Pocket Full of Miracles: A Collection of Heart-warming True Stories*).

Even when we don't know exactly what to say, if the words we utter reflect the feelings of our hearts, the strength of our character, and the depth of our testimony, then the Lord will help us. President Monson promised us that "whom the Lord calls, the Lord qualifies" (*Live the Good Life*, 121).

I will never forget two sisters. It was a dark, dark night in the heart of London. So dark that they were nervous. A man came up by them at the bus stop, a very large man from an even more foreign land than England, and they were more nervous. And then they said they remembered what President Pinegar had once paraphrased for them: "Don't fear, the Lord is before your face. He's on your right hand, he's on your left hand, His Spirit is in your heart, His angels round about you" (see D&C 84:88). So these two sister missionaries spoke. "Excuse me sir, would you be so kind and friendly as to answer a few questions that might bring you happiness?"

And he said, "Well, I'd be glad to young ladies." And he did. He was from the Solomon Islands. He was in England for four weeks. He heard the message and, since the sisters cannot teach a man alone, they went to the church. And later this man, Peter Salaka, said, "I want to meet your president." So I went with them on a discussion. Peter Salaka is an elect man of God—just like we learn in the Doctrine and Covenants, that the elect shall hear his voice and know that it's true (see D&C 29:7). These two sisters taught him. We arranged for a baptism. Peter Salaka spoke at his own baptism. It was the greatest talk I've ever heard at a baptism. It was like he was a bishop already, like he'd been in the Church all of his life. I thought, *Who is this man?*

He was taken to church on Sunday, interviewed, and ordained to the office of a priest after having the Aaronic Priesthood conferred upon him. He then left for the Solomon Islands, which was in one of the Australian missions at the time. I called the Australian mission president and informed him of the baptism of Peter Salaka, who lived in the Solomon Islands. He said, "That's great, that's part of our mission; I think we have one member there on that island. We'll see what we can do."

I said, "Just make sure you make contact with him; I've given him your name, your phone number, and your address. Here's his address back in the Solomon Islands; please write him and follow up. I'll do the same." Time went by, and Elder Sonnenberg of the

Quorum of the Seventy, who was the President of the Australian area, and Elder Faust went on a visit to the Solomon Islands to see what they could do to start the branches there. Peter Salaka greeted them at the airport. "I am Peter Salaka, and this is my son. I am a priest in The Church of Jesus Christ of Latter-day Saints. How can I help you build up the Church here?" Elder Sonnenberg sent me a picture of Elder Faust, himself, and Brother Salaka. Where would he be if those two magnificent sisters had not opened their mouths? If we allow one person to walk by and not open our mouth, we might put off their chance to find hope and peace, and an opportunity for exaltation at that time. And we never know when it might be almost critical that we provide such a chance right then. This isn't a business; this is a matter of spiritual life and death. I am grateful that those faithful sisters opened their mouths so that they could be the instruments in the Lord's hands to bless that great brother.

We must open our mouths and do personal contacting on a daily basis. Make it your goal to open your mouth with every single person you see or come in contact with. "Excuse me, would you be so kind . . . ?" Do not be afraid. You never know who will be a golden contact; you would never want to judge who that might be. But if you're dedicated, the Lord will help you find them.

## Conclusion

Overcoming our many fears is as simple as trusting in the Lord and then attaining whatever preparation lies in our power. One sister explains how she simply put her foot down against fear by simply gaining a little preparation and faith. She had fears of teaching and proselyting; fears of how her home would be cared for; and fears about the well-being of her children to how she would adjust to living in Kenya. Here is what she had to say when she finally faced them with faith:

> I worked at the MTC as a part-time role player. The situations helped me hear what missionaries say—even better, how they bore their own testimonies and were themselves, and it was good.

I talked with experienced senior missionaries and got ideas from them and calmed down. I stored stuff in the attic and decided to let things break or get dusty or dirty. It was part of my gift as a missionary.

Preparations have been made for us, and the Church wants more missionaries to go, so they will do all possible to keep us healthy, etc.

[Regarding her nine children and their spouses and eighteen grandchildren] Remember they are the Lord's—plus, they are adults and can take care of themselves.

—Sister Linda Erickson

And finally, a senior missionary expressed her feelings concerning how the Lord helped them overcome their fears:

We have enjoyed this day and the many things we have learned here at the MTC. The last few months have been a nightmare. I have worried so much about this mission I had agreed to go on. I just knew I could not do it. When I went to be set apart by President Stanley Johnson, he said, "When I get through, you will not have any more fear." As soon as he put his hands on my head I felt my hands, arms, and feet tingle, and I felt lifted up like an angel. I have no more worries. I am well satisfied. I feel like I can conquer the world.

—Sister Peay

These wonderful couples and sisters are not prophets—they are just like you and me with earlier availability dates on their mission papers! Let us follow their examples, just as they have followed others' examples before them. And remember, they are no braver than you are—the Spirit is the key. After you have increased your faith, love, knowledge, preparation, and experience, you will, through your prayers, be comforted and strengthened by the power of the Spirit. Let us all move forward in preparing ourselves to serve with faith in the Lord's work!

# CHAPTER 7

## KNOWING THE ROPES: FEELING

## COMFORTABLE IN YOUR NEW CALLING

Missionary work is like life. It is multifaceted as well as multidimensional. You do a variety of things, but all of it is focused on blessing lives—just plain ol' sharing the gospel, building up the kingdom of God, and making people happy.

As senior missionaries in the field, you will not be required to do the same activities as the younger missionaries. You will be encouraged to set your own pace and your own goals. The missionary rules for the younger missionaries simply do not always apply. For example, you are not normally required to memorize the missionary discussions, but simply to give them in your own words. Or, on your mission should you need more rest, you just take more rest. And as couples, you will stay with your same companion throughout your whole mission. Isn't that nice? You must just use good judgement and not overdo it. As King Benjamin taught us, do not run faster than you have strength (see Mosiah 4:27).

The following chapter outlines some of the activities that senior missionaries get to do, what your goals should be, and how to go about becoming experts in your new comfort zone. Basically, it will show you the ropes to successful senior missionary work!

## Doing Good Continually

People will not listen to your message until they know that they are loved; and then, when they will listen, they will feel the Spirit.

How do we let people know they are loved? By "doing good continually" (see Mosiah 5:2). Be involved in the community wherever possible. Senior missionaries are encouraged to give four hours of Christian service weekly. Some may or may not be able to do that, but wherever possible be active in the community. Do everything you can so that the image of Christ is not only in your countenance, but is expressed through your service to the community in which you reside. Then you'll touch hearts and make friends that you can share the gospel with. If it is appropriate (for your particular neighborhood), become a part of the neighborhood where you live to let them know that you are part of the community.

Always keep the lines of communication open with the ward or branch leaders. Secure a ward or branch list so you can visit people when time permits. This is because it's important to remember the scripture in John 15:16, that the fruit of gospel seeds might remain. It is important as we work in the fellowship area to make everyone feel loved—old members, new members, investigating members, less-active members. Pay special attention to those that might be struggling. When new people move in, make sure they feel welcome and that you extend your love to them.

It is wonderful to fellowship people and let them know they are loved and needed, for we are all a community of Saints. You can even volunteer to be a part of the coordinating effort for this, to make yourself available to help new converts become firmly rooted in the gospel—as directed by your branch or ward leaders. (We must always remember to support the leaders and sustain them in all that they do.)

Be an example to others. You might even ask the bishop or branch president for several older couples or senior sisters that you could train to be fellowshippers and friendshippers. Fellowshippers are those who help the new converts, and friendshippers are those who help the new investigators. Both roles are very important.

One exciting thing about missionary work as full-time missionaries, even though your assignment may be office or humanitarian or welfare or temple or whatever it might be, is that there is always time to bless people's lives. There is always time to home teach or visit teach a person in your off-duty time. Or just make social, loving visits to the people who are already hearing the discussions. This way you can constantly renew the joy that Alma described of helping others come unto Christ.

One way you can do this is to go between the teaching appointments of the sisters and elders. So if you are working in a district, or even in an office, or wherever you are, you can call up the zone leader and ask, "Who is in our area that we could just visit and say hello to?" Then find out what discussion they are on, and visit them and take them some cookies or bring them a little treat, and they'll just love to be loved.

Or, it's always fun to share any Church literature that you may have—an *Ensign*, a *Friend*, the *New Era*, some pamphlets, and of course, the Book of Mormon. Whenever you can, write your testimony in the Book of Mormon and place it with someone, obtaining a promise to read and a call-back appointment. If nothing else, you'll be sowing seeds in that garden of love, and people will remember how you treated them.

President Spallino, of the England Birmingham Mission, said he can still remember the feelings he had for the couple missionaries serving when he was a young elder 25 years ago. "I was in Italy and these couples could not speak the language, but I remember the love they could give, and the [people] felt that love" (*Church News,* 14 Sept. 1996).

## Working with the Members

Don't overlook the power of working with members to find new investigators. If you want extra power, delegation is a great tool for getting things accomplished. God the Father delegated the creation of the earth to His Son, Jehovah. Jehovah also delegated and went down with Michael and others, and *they* organized this earth from material that had always existed. Then, under the ultimate *direction* of the Father, our first parents were created.

I believe in delegation; I believe that many hands make light work. If I were on a mission, I would work with members in the ward or branch where I was serving. I'd find five or ten people, and I'd develop relationships of trust with them. I'd visit them, get to know them, prove my righteousness, and let them see my sincere desire. That would convince them to be a part of the missionary effort.

You should also help members work within their wards to strengthen those already struggling to endure to the end. Always volunteer to be a home teacher—and you can go together as companions. Or in the case of senior sisters serving as missionaries, you can be visiting teachers. Just make sure you are available to fellowship and help the new converts and the less-active members within the ward or branch in which you serve. Sometimes in wards a brother might be asked to serve as branch president and the sister might serve as the Relief Society president while on their mission. Or you just might be asked to be a shadow leader or mentor. Whatever it is you're asked to do, the joy is in helping people do better in that which they have been called to do, and in being able to strengthen them in all your conversation, in all your prayers, in all your doings, and in all your exhortations. Just reread Doctrine and Covenants 108:7 to remind yourself how you can strengthen others at all times.

One fun way to strengthen the Church is to teach the members; for teaching is the greatest thing you'll ever do. Teach them what you're doing as missionaries, or, where needed, how to hold family home evenings, how to have family activities, how to start a family reunion, or how to start family history research. You can even volunteer to teach the Gospel Essentials class, or a special class within the ward or branch. You can do so many things. Some welfare missionaries simply teach cleanliness and nutrition. You can teach English as a second language. Just teach whatever you can in the unit that you're serving in.

One thing that is really wonderful is to work with the younger people of the ward. Be involved with the Primary and the Young Men and Young Women, and you will inspire them to serve missions. Remember that every time you help a person to serve a mission it means that, in time, thousands of people are blessed—maybe even hundreds of thousands are blessed through genealogical research. The important thing is that we are in the business to help people come unto Christ. And it really becomes wonderful as we see the fruits of our labors.

## Working with Younger Missionaries

Another exciting thing in the mission field is that as a member of a zone or district you will have the opportunity to work with the young men and women missionaries, and this is a great time to be a mentor—a father or mother figure to homesick or otherwise in-need sisters and elders in the zone.

You can also strengthen the missionary effort by teaming up and providing a more effective peer group for investigators. Wherever possible, you could even go on a "teach" with the younger missionaries. It's okay if four people go along sometimes to give added strength, especially if the individual the younger missionaries are teaching is older, because investigators then have the opportunity of sharing concerns with a teacher who might more closely relate to their experiences.

Even though you will take direction from the younger missionaries, they have been directed to be very sensitive to your needs and concerns. Plus, you'll get to teach them how to lead—it's the only chance the younger missionaries have ever had at leading and directing a mature couple or sister. I always enjoyed it when the zone leader would ask me, "How do I lead the senior missionaries?"

I would simply answer, "Ask them if they would be so kind as to do the following . . . and then explain why."

"Is that all?" they would ask.

I responded with a simple, "Yes," having already instructed the senior missionaries on how to help the young missionaries be their district and zone leaders (my little secret). It was then simply delightful to watch the relationship between the senior missionaries and their leaders develop.

Some couples have commented on how tickled they were to work with the younger missionaries, "Oh President, I love my zone leader so much. He's so kind and so tender. He's like a loving son, and I do everything he asks me to do. We really have a wonderful relationship." Those are some of the feelings that have been expressed to me as a mission president in regard to senior couples dealing with the younger missionaries.

## Your Physical Well-Being

It is important that you not only eat properly, but eat the proper foods, including any supplements you may feel you need. For those who take medicines, stay up on them. Along with that, it is a must to exercise and walk regularly whenever you can. And above all, get adequate rest. As senior missionaries we need more rest. And again, as mentioned earlier, do not run faster than you have strength.

It is important that you be strong; remember that if you are sick, your companion is sick, for you are one. So be strong physically and safeguard your health in every way. And should you get any feelings of sickness or be involved in an accident, call the mission president immediately so that the right place and the right doctor can be found so as to ensure that you're in good health and strength. It's important as missionaries that we take care of our health, for if we're not healthy we cannot preach the word or do our duties.

## A Carpetbag of Cautions

- We must be careful to avoid counseling or dealing with people's personal problems. Always seek out the branch president, bishop, or stake president for those things.

- In regard to finances, it is important to always be up to date on your bills and be careful not to loan money—even to other missionaries. There is a program for missionary funds set up through the mission president; this way there are never any hard feelings or misunderstandings. Always let the mission president take care of financial difficulties. And if you are aware of missionaries who might be having financial difficulties, a telephone call or a letter to the mission president to make him aware of the problem is an appropriate thing to do.

- In regard to your personal property, many missionaries leave behind gifts with people in the area, but as to the use of your own car, it is highly advised not to lend your car or allow others to drive it, for you are personally, legally, and financially responsible.

- Always be aware of the local culture. Be sure never to do anything that would disrespect their customs, traditions, shrines, or anything of that nature.

- As to your dress, be neat and tidy, not flamboyant or dragging about heavy jewelry. Be conservative in all that you do. Look your best. Look like you represent the Lord Jesus Christ.

- A caution never to forget: never ever be alone with anyone of the opposite sex, other than your spouse, because too many things can go wrong—you're just asking for rumors, innuendos, and accusations. These insinuations, no matter how untrue, cause nothing but problems for you, the Church, and the missionary effort.

- As you teach people, it is important that you are always in a positive, enthusiastic, upbeat mode, and never get into debates, arguments, or contention of any kind. It is important you be careful in both your demeanor and your relationships with others so that you come across in a pleasant, outstanding way—you are always representing our Savior Jesus Christ and the Church.

## Expect Quiet Fulfillment

We must go into this kind of work expecting quiet fulfillment. We don't receive worldly glory and honor as we strive to create little Zions in the homes of those we teach and in our own hearts. The prophet Ezra Taft Benson has taught us clearly about the rewards of missionary service.

> Render Christlike service. Christlike service exalts. Knowing this, we call upon all senior members who are able to thrust in their sickles in service to others. This can be part of the sanctifying process. The Lord has promised that those who lose their lives serving others will find themselves. The Prophet Joseph Smith told us that we should "wear out our lives" in bringing to pass His purposes [see D&C 123:13].

Peace and joy and blessings will follow those who render service to others. Yes, we commend Christlike service to all, but it is especially sweet in the lives of the elderly (*Come, Listen to a Prophet's Voice,* 71).

Elder Hales stressed the blessing of togetherness and growth as a source of fulfillment in missionary work. He said:

The blessings of serving with your eternal companion are priceless and can only be understood by those who have experienced it. My wife and I have had that privilege in the mission field. Each day is a special day with daily rewards that cause personal growth and development in the Lord's time and in the Lord's way. The fulfillment that comes from this kind of service will bless you, your marriage, and your family for eternity (*Ensign,* May 2001, 27).

Finally, Elder Spencer J. Condie reminds us that our work will not go unnoticed, and that it does make a difference in our lives and others' lives.

And finally, in our heart of hearts we must sometimes confess that we are more willing to serve as a stake president than as a home teacher, or more ready to be a mission president than to serve as a senior missionary couple in a small remote branch near the end of the earth. Mission presidents and their wives have their pictures published in the Church News, but missionary couples serve rather anonymously throughout the world. And a loving Father in Heaven has great blessings in store for them, and grateful mission presidents will praise their names for all the good they do, for their initiative and their obedience (*In Perfect Balance,* 121).

But not only do senior couples make a difference just today and in individual lives, but their efforts will some day have made the difference for whole continents, and for generations of families in the world to come. Even now, some senior couples have activated whole congregations while others strengthened feeble branches into what are now thriving wards. In a number of other countries, it was couples who helped pave the way for the Church to gain legal status.

Elder L. Tom Perry, of the Quorum of the Twelve, referred to this significant service of older missionaries in general conference:

> You are the ones who can build a first root structure, which will support the new converts in the truths of the gospel in this life and help them become worthy to receive the blessings in the eternities to come. . . .
>
> To you who will accept the call to go forth and serve, I can promise you that your good name will never be forgotten in this world or in the eternities to come (*Church News,* 15 Aug. 1992, 3).

## Conclusion

Keep these things in mind as you prepare to create your new comfort zone. Work hard to love and serve and maintain a positive attitude. Always follow whatever mission rules you are given—keeping yourself in the bounds that draw protection from heaven. Remember foremost that you are a representative of the Savior and His Church, and that you will be an example to missionaries you serve with, the units that you work in, and generations to come—especially an example of love. And those seeds of example will eventually grow into a vast garden, and you will reap the harvest of many grateful souls in this life, and find that multiplied in the next with many happy greetings.

# CHAPTER 8

## BLESSINGS OF THE SPIRIT

The Spirit is an essential part of missionary work because it is what truly converts people to the gospel. It also compensates for all the flaws of our less-than-perfect presentation of the gospel. We may think, "I'm not ready, I don't know how to do this, how can I ever do it?" The Lord and the Spirit will assist you. "I will go before your face. I will be on your right hand and on your left, and my Spirit shall be in your hearts, and mine angels round about you, to bear you up" (D&C 84:88). The Lord is there helping every missionary, every day, by the power of the Spirit. We are simply instruments for the Lord— a conduit for the Spirit. Every week or so I get letters from missionaries. They say, "Oh Brother Ed, it's just like you said, it's so great, I feel the Spirit and I'm so happy. We just baptized. The Lord is so good to us in our trials as well as our successes."

Having the Spirit on our missions does make the good in life override the trials. We feel successful because we are—whether with an investigator or just in strengthening our own ties to the Lord. We need never fear our responsibilities if we remain worthy of the Spirit. The Lord is, indeed, good to us. He has promised that "the Comforter, which is the Holy Ghost . . . shall teach [us] all things, and bring all things to [our] remembrance, whatsoever [He has] said unto [us]" (John 14:26).

# Having the Spirit in Your Companionship

Before you can hope to introduce others to the Spirit you must have it—as a companionship! As husband and wife, you have undoubtedly learned that having the Spirit in your marriage is a key ingredient to accomplishing much good. However, we all know that the Spirit of Christ does not linger in an atmosphere of hostility or unkind words. Three ways to keep the Spirit in our companionships—as well as in our teaching environments—are to express love, build trust and accept loving feedback, and use the Spirit's words, not the world's.

## Express Love

You can save yourselves a lot of problems during this earth life by expressing the love of God and the love of Christ through communication. Whether it be verbal, by touch, or by whatever means, please communicate your love (see John 13:34–35). I know it takes time and effort, but nothing else you do during your mission will bring greater rewards. And without expressing your love, true communication simply won't occur.

When my daughter Tricia was a young girl she'd wait for me to get home every night. When I'd come in the door she would greet me with, "Hi, Daddy, I love ya!" My heart warmed, I smiled, and my burdens were lifted. I was then in a good mood, less defensive, and ready to face the challenges of home life with a soft heart.

Start the process now of working with yourself and with your companion on learning to express your love for each other and the great work that you are doing together.

## Build Trust and Accept Loving Feedback

When trying to build strong communication patterns, one of the most difficult things to incorporate is being able to accept when we're doing something that may not be perfect, to be given counsel on it, and to admit that everyone else can see it except us. Let me tell you how it started in our family.

"Sweetheart," my wife said to me one day, "I think we need to take time to evaluate our lives and see how we're doing." So we had our first big evaluation (we call it "companionship inventory").

We sat down and I said, "Honey, how are you doing? How am I doing? What could I work on?"

"Oh you're fine, sweetheart," she answered. "But it might be nice if you'd work a little more in the yard."

"What do you mean?" I bristled. *I've been slaving in mouths* (I'm a dentist), *filling cavities, taking out wisdom teeth—foraging in the field for food—and you're worried about whether or not I'm working in the yard!?* I didn't say that, but I thought that.

I simply wasn't ready to accept any constructive criticism. Accepting feedback requires a person to say, "Tell me what I can change; I am ready and open and willing to listen." It almost takes the courage of David because our hearts are so very sensitive and vulnerable. My wife can tell me anything now, and I'm so grateful because we have a relationship in which I can say, "Sweetheart . . ." and she understands what I'm trying to communicate. The other day I was having a tough day, feeling a little sick and weak and powerless. I came into the house, found my darling wife, and said, "Sweetheart . . ." I was totally exhausted and I wanted to go to sleep, yet I knew I couldn't. She saw that, heard the plea in my voice, and gave me a hug.

"Honey, I just need some strength," I said. "I'm getting weak." I felt her strength in that hug pouring into me, sustaining me, and carrying me through the rest of the day. She understood my troubles, and loved and supported me with the love of Christ. She didn't say, "Why don't you do this?" or "Why don't you do that?" She didn't find fault with me or scold my weakness. She simply loved me because we share a deep trust in our relationship. It's so wonderful now when my wife says, "Sweetheart, it would really help if you would . . ." And I can answer, "Oh honey, thank you, I'll be so much better." Accepting feedback is the essence of humility.

After we have a relationship of trust in our communication, we have enough humility to say, "OK, tell me because I want to grow." If we have an insatiable desire to be like the Savior, people can say, "Hey, you've got to change . . ."

And we'll be able to answer, "OK, OK, I'll be better." As missionaries, when you can do that, you will change, and the communication in your companionship will be open, candid, and honest. But remember that you can only do this when you are willing and ready to do it.

### Use the Spirit's Words, Not the World's

We can only communicate honestly if we are led by the Spirit—in other words, when we ask ourselves in every situation, "What would Jesus do?" and "How would the Spirit direct us?" If any of you were to say, "President, I need to see you" and then come in for an interview, long before you ever walked in the door I would have already prayed: "Father, what would Thou have me say if Thou were here at this very moment?"

Our communication must be honest and open, but it must also be kind and sensitive. One good brother counseled his daughter as to how to balance her honesty with sensitivity. He told her, "Always ask yourself if what you are about to say is true, if it's necessary, *and* if it's kind." If we consider kindness, chances are we will always be led by the Spirit, and that is vital in preventing hurt feelings. Communication is a powerful way of helping or harming others; while we can choose whether to let words hurt us, we cannot choose how our words will affect others—and they really can hurt more than sticks or stones.

Along with this same carefulness in addressing others directly, we should also watch the tone of our general conversations and statements—especially as missionaries! So often our communication is flippant, light-minded, casual, and worldly. It seems that everything now has to be fun or funny. In chapters 37, 38, and 42 of the book of Alma, the prophet Alma counsels his sons to teach the word with soberness. I'm not saying we can't laugh (I love to laugh as much as anyone else), but there's a right time and a right place.

Sober-mindedness is one of the most essential traits in order to be a spiritual giant, in order to speak by the Spirit, to be led by the Spirit, to be Ammon-like and Alma-like missionaries. The language we use is an important key in maintaining sober-mindedness. We need to communicate the way the Spirit communicates—with love, tenderness, and sensitivity, as well as appropriately.

## Allowing the Spirit to Convert

As missionaries, there is one thing that we must understand: the Spirit converts, not us. With that in mind, we must do all we can do to foster an environment where the Spirit can be present, and then just allow it to convert those we have taught. Elder Loren C. Dunn said:

> There is something unique about the work of the Church that rests within the souls of those who have come into the gate of faith in Christ, repentance, and baptism. It is born of the Spirit of the Lord and takes us beyond the knowledge that the Church is true. It is a matter of the heart and of the soul, and it has the capacity to change us like nothing else can. It is the spirit of conversion, and it is at the center of this great latter-day work. It has the power to change people's hearts and bring them to Christ through repentance and baptism. It has the power to draw people into the kingdom of God and make of them new people ("The Spirit of Conversion," *Ensign,* July 2000, 7).

## Invoking and Keeping the Spirit

Invoking the Spirit may be one of the most challenging things to do as a missionary, but when you find the way that works best for you, the results are glorious. Your love for your companion and those you teach is increased, and the gospel message is transmitted through the Spirit.

There are many ways to invoke the Spirit in your interactions with investigators. Take the time to read the Book of Mormon with your investigators. In our family, when our kids were growing up, we read the Book of Mormon out loud for years. I remember when the children first started; they thought I was a crazy, bald, senile old man, and I probably was, but later they saw the value of reading the scriptures every day. As the younger children were born, they didn't know anything else but scripture time. I remember they became so excited to get their copies of the Book of Mormon with their names on them, and their red pencils to underline important passages. And when we read the Book of Mormon, we would read aloud. Tonight at ten o'clock I'll be propped up in bed with my wife and we'll read again out of the scriptures. Why so much reading? Because it helps us feel the spirit.

Janet Thomas explains this beautifully.

> The day after planting corn, Rachel was stiff and sore, but she knew that the good feelings she got from service would last longer than the pain. She was also able to compare her repeated days in the garden to the scriptures. "We had talked about he lasting effects of service and how you feel the effects of what you do for a long time after. . . . It was like when you read the scriptures and feel the Spirit. Eventually the feeling goes away, so the only way you can keep having [it] is by going back and reading more and more" ("Good Seed," *New Era,* Nov. 1995, 23).

Read the scriptures aloud with your contacts so they'll feel the Spirit and desire to act on those good feelings (see Gal. 5:22–23; D&C 11:12–13).

Another way to invoke the Spirit is to show your investigators that you love them. Assist them in every way, temporally and spiritually. If they're busy and they can't hear a discussion and their boys are playing soccer, well what should we do, elders and sisters? Let's go see the soccer game, of course. That's a great teaching moment. You're their friend and you care about what they care about. You can do all kinds of good things. But you let the families know that you love and care about them. Make regular contact—either in person, through a member, with a note, with a card, with a telephone call, with whatever it might be, and make sure you drop off some chocolate chip cookies. Make regular contacts of love. When you contact people it shows you care. These contacts can remind investigators how the

Spirit feels and refreshes their memory about the great commitments they are keeping. In Doctrine and Covenants 76: 116 we learn that the "power of the Holy Spirit" is bestowed by God "on those who love him." Surely love brings the Spirit, which brings conversion and commitment.

Make church attendance high on the list in preparing your investigators for conversion and baptism. We often feel the Spirit at church as the Lord promised us: "Where two or three are gathered together in my name, there am I in the midst of them" (Matt. 18:20). The more that people attend church, the more they'll have their hearts touched and their desires changed. Then they'll be more likely to make and keep all the commitments that help us become good members of the Church.

## Identifying and Teaching with the Spirit

People can feel the Spirit all of their life, but until they recognize and identify it, they will not know its source or the good that it can cause in their lives when they act upon those promptings. Once investigators feel the Spirit, you can ask things such as, "How do you feel when we teach you these things?" or "How did you feel when you read the Book of Mormon?" or "How did you feel when you attended church?" They may respond by saying something to the effect of, "I feel love, peace, joy, long-suffering, gentleness, goodness, faith, meekness, and temperance" (see Galatians 5:22–23), or "I had a desire to do good, to do justly, to walk humbly. My mind was enlightened and I made a good judgment. I felt joy" (see D&C 11:12–13). These are the feelings of the Spirit. And when someone feels the Spirit, we must identify it as such so they understand how the Spirit speaks to them. When they know that, then they start to understand how the Spirit will teach and witness to them the truth of the gospel.

After they recognize the Spirit, we can ask our investigators to commit to do something because the Spirit will touch their hearts and make them willing to change and have faith. The words you will use to help them make those commitments are *will you*. For example, "Will you read the Book of Mormon? Will you pray about the

Church (or about Joseph being the prophet of the Restoration, or about the truthfulness of the Book of Mormon)? Will you try to keep the Word of Wisdom?" The words *will you* are the key to helping people make and keep commitments; and people change and are converted no faster than they make and keep those commitments.

I promised the elders and sisters in the mission, "If you get more than five investigators past the third discussion, I will come any night, every night of my life in England, and teach—give a fireside or a cottage meeting."

Well, Elder Gaskell and his companion in the Guilford ward had five. They called me up, "President, we've got five."

I was so excited. I can still remember my talk; it was on 2 Peter—taking upon yourself the divine nature of Christ (1:3–12). After the talk, I walked down and started to visit with the investigators. I said, "Debbie, it's so good to be with you, and I'm so glad that you were here tonight. It was nice to meet you." I asked, "How did you feel?"

She said, "Oh, so good!"

I said, "Well, how do you feel when the elders teach you?"

"Oh, I just want to be good."

I said, "You know that's the Spirit?"

She said, "Yes, and I feel that at church too."

I said, "How do you feel about the Book of Mormon?"

"Oh, I love to read it."

I asked, "How do you feel about its truthfulness?"

"Oh, I know it's true." And then all of a sudden the Spirit spoke to me and said that she was ready.

I said, "Debbie, you know this week I'm fairly busy, but on Thursday night I have some time. *Will you* be baptized Thursday night?"

She said, "Why yes President, I'd be glad to be baptized. Will you baptize me?"

I answered excitedly, "Oh Debbie, I'll be glad to baptize you." She felt the Spirit so she was willing to commit.

Then Debbie told me that Sister Choate and Brother Choate had been coming along quite nicely. So I said to Sister Choate, "Debbie mentioned that you've enjoyed the missionaries."

"Oh yes, I love the Book of Mormon. I love going to church."

Then I responded, "Sister Choate, then you felt that feeling of wanting to do good and follow Christ, and when you come to know that these things are true, do you want to follow Christ and be baptized?"

"Oh yes, I feel that way President Pinegar."

At that point I told her about Debbie being baptized on Thursday night and asked her if she would be willing to be baptized Thursday night as well. She said, "Why yes, I would love to. Will you baptize me?"

I told her I'd be tickled to do that. But then she told me that Brother Choate was having a little trouble with tithing. So I spoke to her good husband. "Brother Choate, your beautiful wife has mentioned that she's excited and wants to be baptized Thursday. She mentioned that you struggle a little bit with the principle of tithing."

He answered frankly, "Well, yes."

Then I said, "Brother Choate, I want to bear you my testimony. I promise you that if you pay your tithing, because you know that this Church is true, I promise you that your finances will be alright, and things will work out, and the Lord will bless you. If you will make and keep this commitment, you can covenant with the Lord and come into His Church."

He said, "President Pinegar, I'll be baptized."

Well now I was just on cloud nine. They were having squash and biscuits (that's punch and cookies in England), so I walked up and asked Elder Gaskell if he thought he could work out a baptism for Thursday.

And he asked, "Oh, who's being baptized?" When I told him it was Debbie and Brother and Sister Choate, he wanted to know how I knew that and who had asked them.

I said, "Elder Gaskell, I did. Is that alright?"

"Well, how did you do that?" he asked.

So I told him. "Elder Gaskell, I simply asked, 'Will you be baptized?' and they said 'yes,' because they felt the Spirit." He just looked at me. And the baptisms were wonderful. The bishop and the home teachers and visiting teachers were there. It was wonderful!

The Spirit also gives us courage to persist if our investigators want to stop receiving the discussions. With the Spirit, we may have the courage to say, "Oh please, won't you listen one more time?" They often won't listen until they see your true concern, but when they see and feel your concern for them, you will have the power to awaken their souls to God. You will have *savor*. Do you know what savor is? In the Doctrine and Covenants we read:

> When men [and women] are called unto mine everlasting gospel, and covenant with an everlasting covenant [and we've done that], they are accounted as the salt of the earth and the savor of men;
>
> They are called to be the savor of men; therefore, if that salt [you and me] of the earth lose its savor, behold, it is thenceforth good for nothing only to be cast out and trodden under the feet of men (101:39-40).

In other words, to be "the salt of the earth" and "the savor of men" means to have the power to awaken people to God. But if we don't desire to do this, we'll lose our savor and never have this power and influence.

When you have the salt within you and the savor is in your soul, the Spirit will do its part. As Nephi tells us, if you have desire, despite your weaknesses, the power of the Spirit will carry truth unto the hearts of your investigators and the less-active members you meet (2 Ne. 33:1).

## Being Led by the Spirit

Nephi is a supreme example of being led by the Spirit. You will recall that as he returned to Jerusalem to retrieve the brass plates (an undoubtedly perilous journey!) he noted that he was "led by the Spirit, not knowing beforehand the things which I should do" (1 Ne. 4:6). Nephi acknowledges that he didn't know how to get the plates, but he drew upon a major source of guidance—the Spirit.

Sometimes as missionaries we get nervous about what we're going to say or how we'll know the best response to a situation. We can take comfort in the words of the Doctrine and Covenants: "Treasure up in your minds continually the words of life, and it shall be given you in the very hour that portion that shall be meted unto every man" (84:85). "For it shall be given you in the very hour, yea, in the very moment, what ye shall say" (D&C 100:6). The Lord is with you when you are a missionary (see D&C 84:86–88). The key for all this to happen, as missionaries, is to have the Spirit. For without the Spirit, you cannot preach, you cannot teach, you cannot understand, and you cannot be led. The Spirit is the key. And with the Spirit you can do all things because the Spirit will direct you. It is the Spirit that will convert.

Let me illustrate these points with an experience I had some years ago. It was about 1969 when a young girl named Susan Gerszewski came to see me. "Bishop, you've got to take my name off the records of the Church."

I said, "Oh Susan, what's wrong?"

"My brothers think I'm a dork for being here at BYU, and I can't stand the pressure when I go home, and my parents are wondering what's gone wrong with me."

And then all of a sudden, the Lord stepped in and words came out of my mouth like this: "Susan, I promise you that if you stay faithful, your brothers will join the Church and your parents' hearts will soften." Now how could I say that? I couldn't. Only the Lord could.

She said, "Oh, I just don't know Bishop, I just don't know."

I said, "Well Susan, is the Book of Mormon true?"

"Well, of course it is Bishop."

"Do you love the Savior and do you believe in Heavenly Father?"

"Yes I do."

"Is the prophet the head of the Church today?"

"Of course."

"Is this the true Church?"

"Of course it is. But I just can't stand the pressure."

I said, "Susan, will you be willing to try, because the Lord just gave you a promise."

She said, "Well, I guess I can try." That year she moved out of the ward and I lost track of her.

Well, at BYU in 1972 I volunteered to teach another religion class, besides the Book of Mormon, before going to my dental office. It was the Gospel Principles and Practices class. There were about sixty students in the class, and life was going just merrily along, and on the last day to drop the class, this student came up to me and said, "I've got to drop your class."

I asked, "How come?"

He said, "Well, I'm on scholarship, and if I don't get a B or a B+ I could lose my scholarship; and I got a C+ on the test, and besides I'm not a Mormon."

I looked at his little information sheet I had him fill out before class, and I'd missed it. He'd checked "nonmember" so close to the "member" that I'd missed it.

I said, "Well Jim, you mean you're just afraid you won't get a B?"

He said, "Well, how can I? I'm not a member, and I just can't risk it."

I said, "Jim I've got an idea. Do you normally study once a week for this class?"

He answered, "Yes."

I said, "Jim, I've got it. Would you mind studying with me Tuesday nights for an hour before class on Wednesday?"

He said, "Yes, but what will that do?"

I continued, "Well Jim, you want a B, right? Do you know who makes out the grade?"

He answered, "Well, you do."

I smiled. "That's right Jim; I'm guaranteeing you a B or a B+."

"You mean you'll guaran . . . "

"I guarantee it. Look, I'm going to teach you extra Tuesday nights. If you're in my house for an hour, well, I'll make up the test too. I'll even help you prepare for the test. Jim I'm guaranteeing you this."

Jim said, "Well that's a deal, I'm going to study with you." So Jim came up to my house, and this went on for a couple of weeks, and then one day he asked, "Hey Brother Ed, could I bring my brother and my roommate up? I mean, we have banana splits and root beer floats and doughnuts every time I come up; we might as well invite others and have parties when you teach."

And so I said, "You bet, you bring them up." So we went along for four more weeks, and then this one night they came up and they were kind of kidding around a lot, so I said, "You guys are sure having a hoot tonight. What's up around here?"

They looked at each other as if to say, "OK, who's going to tell him," and then Jim finally said, "Brother Ed, we've been thinking, and we talked to our bishop, and we all want to be baptized, and will you baptize us and confirm us members of the Church next week?"

As I floated down from the ceiling I said, "Yes Jim. I will, I will, I will." Well, his name was Jim Gerszewski, but I had mispronounced his name. Jim was Susan's brother; Susan was at the baptism, and joy was felt by all.

Now you tell me that God our Father and Jesus Christ are not in charge of everything on this earth. How could those words come out of my mouth, "Your brothers will join the Church"? How, two years later, could one of those brothers be in my class? There were 20,000 students at BYU then. Don't tell me that the Lord's hand isn't in all things that are good. All three boys served missions. All three were married in the temple. And Jim's roommate Larry Kacher went on to serve as a mission president in Geneva, Switzerland—all those fruits from just trusting in the Spirit!

The Spirit "will show unto you all things what ye should do" (2 Ne. 32:5). Why is this so important? Because the vision in missionary work is that you must prepare yourself and those you teach to feel the Spirit. Their needs are individual, and sometimes only the Spirit can tell you those needs. Once those needs are discerned, you can respond to them with the Spirit and in the way the Lord would have you.

## Conclusion

Do you see why no amount of rhetoric or skillful manipulation can ever replace the Spirit? We don't convert, the Spirit does. Do you see why we simply pray for hearts to be softened? Do you understand why, when we're humble, we can communicate? The only way that we ever reach the point of getting down to the most basic level is when heart speaks to heart through and by the Spirit. We can give an eloquent message of the gospel, but the only way that it will enter *into* the hearts of those we teach is by the Spirit. Its workings in our own lives and in the lives of those we teach are marvelous. It allows us to teach as the Lord would have us teach, be led and lead others unto Him, and it enriches the relationships with those around us. The key is understanding how to obtain it in our lives, and in our teaching, and how to use it for the building up of His kingdom here on the earth.

# CHAPTER 9

## UNDERSTANDING THE IMPORTANCE OF
## RETENTION AND ACTIVATION

For Heavenly Father's children to gain eternal life they must come into the Church. They must be baptized, but being baptized is not enough. They must endure to the end. We learn in John 15:16 that the Savior was praying that the Apostles' fruit might remain—that is, that the Saints, after baptism, would be retained in the kingdom of God. The balanced effort in missionary work is that we should simultaneously emphasize conversion, retention, and activation. In other words, just because people are baptized doesn't mean the work is over. The work with them is forever.

## Finding the Ninety and Nine Plus One

President Gordon B. Hinckley has explained the need for our care and friendliness out in the world, the need for us to be searchers—instruments for good in His hand. Our prophet explains our great need to find those who have lost their way, or to find those who are lost because they haven't yet found their way.

> Your friendly ways are needed. Your sense of responsibility is needed. The Savior of all mankind left the ninety and nine to find the one lost. That one who was lost need not have become lost. But if he is out there somewhere in the shadows, and if it means leaving the ninety and nine, we must do so to find him ("Converts and Young Men," *Ensign*, May 1997, 47).

The lost can be any who need to find the gospel, or to find it again. But how do we go about searching in the shadows; where do we even begin? One of the best ways to make the world a little smaller, to find all of God's children that are ready for the gospel, is to expand our connections by enlisting the help of member missionaries—to ask them to join us in being faith-filled seekers! Every member, in one way or another, is a result of missionary work, and most members have had a missionary experience. They likely understand the importance of making the social connection to the Church and will be a valuable resource in retaining new converts. But sometimes members are as afraid to open their mouths as we were as new missionaries (imagine that!). Even going out of our comfort zones to welcome a new member takes courage. So we, as missionaries, need to tell them how easy it is. Share your own missionary experiences with members. Ask them to share their conversion story with you. Tell them about one of the people you've just recently converted. Tell them about the greatest work in the world. Tell them what a joy it is to work with people who are eager to hear about the gospel. Tell them how wonderful it is to be associated with people who are searching for the truth. As we share these missionary experiences, the Spirit of the Lord will come upon us and inspire us with love of our fellow brothers and sisters. Take advantage of this positive feeling—invite members to reach out to new converts and less-actives.

When investigators, converts, and less-actives are taught in other members' homes, you will be highly successful. So be sure and schedule enough time in your mission to visit members, to inspire them, to love them, to motivate them, to commit them to setting a date to prepare a friend. And you can only do that when they trust you and love you and respect you. You must have the same attitude of patience and love with the members that you do with your investigators. Ask them to help you find people to teach, to help you friendship and fellowship the people you are teaching now.

During a mission presidents' seminar in June of 1980, President Kimball promised Church members that if they would pray night and morning regarding their desire to see other people join the Church, the Lord would hear their prayers and soften the hearts of the people they associate with. Invite your member friends to pray every day for this blessing, and promise them that when they pray with all their hearts, with real intent, they'll see a difference as the hearts of their friends and associates are touched and softened.

Now, for missionaries to get members to do this, we need a relationship of trust with those members. We need to present them a message about the worth of souls, and how important members are in the conversion process—how important it is to friendship and fellowship investigators and new converts. You've got to make sure that the members are converted to loving people, praying for people, and opening their mouths to share this wonderful gospel.

Elder Ballard taught many members on this point. In 1994 he came to the McKay building at the UVSC campus and spoke in a fireside. Eight thousand people were there. He said, "Set a date to find someone to share the gospel with. Set a date and then pray that the Lord will provide you with someone who wants to hear the gospel. You members go out and find people, and the missionaries will teach them."

One brother with whom I am acquainted found a boy by the name of Ty McDonald, and he was baptized; and I thought, *Well, I'm a member too. I've got to find somebody,* so I set a date. And I remember a name came into my mind—Jeff Lewis, he was the one. So I came back from that fireside that week, and I said to my missionary preparation class, "You know, I know just the person, and I've got the date, but I don't know where he is. He was here at UVSC, but he's gone. I haven't seen him for a year." I added, "Jeff Lewis is his name. Do any of you know someone by that name?"

What was the mathematical probability of that happening? A boy in the class raised his hand and said, "Oh, Jeff Lewis? I know him. He's a nonmember. He lives with my best friend down at BYU."

I said, "Are you serious?"

He said, "Yes."

I said, "Can you give me his phone number?"

He said, "Of course."

That week I got Jeff Lewis's phone number and called him. "Jeff, this is Brother Ed."

"Brother Ed, my friend," was his marvelous response. We were friends because I taught him as a nonmember at the institute and he had the discussions, but then he moved. So I had to find him again.

I said, "Jeff, I want to talk to you. Would you be so kind and friendly as to come and see me?" Jeff came out to my office. We visited three times. I challenged him, and he was baptized. On January 12, 1997, I baptized Jeff Lewis at BYU and spoke at his baptism. What if Elder Ballard hadn't spoken? What if I hadn't opened my mouth in class and said, "Who knows Jeff Lewis?" And lo and behold, what did the Lord do? He arranged for somebody to be in class that day; someone who knew where Jeff lived and knew his roommate. And oh, by the way, to make it a little easier for me, He made sure that someone had Jeff's phone number so I could call him.

If we have faith, and exercise that faith by our works—opening our mouths and convincing others to do the same—then the Lord will lead us to His elect and His lost, and He will prepare their hearts. This is a truth we must share with the member missionaries, and remember the prophets have said that's every one of them, so that we all might be a force for good in the Lord's hands.

## Retaining the Converts: Feeding the Lord's Sheep

As missionaries, and as members, we are working together to help bring souls truly to Christ. After their baptism we should always help converts prepare for the temple to be sealed for time and all eternity or to prepare for their missions. We always let people know there's more to the kingdom than just being baptized. We want enduring conversions. They have to acquire a deep and abiding testimony of the gospel of Jesus Christ and the Church.

The baptismal checklist should be used with utmost accuracy, even after your investigator has been baptized. If you follow it—making sure your converts have met the bishop and ward leaders, have had all their interviews and discussions, have set up goals for the temple, etc.—the chances of retention are much higher. As missionaries you should follow up to make sure that everything on the checklist has been taken care of. This involves ensuring that the new convert has an opportunity to receive a calling, and if they are men, an opportunity to receive the priesthood. You should do everything in your power to help them remain active.

## Teach New-Member Discussions

Teach the new-member discussions for newly baptized individuals. And they are easy. They teach basic principles just like those you relearned in chapter two of this book (the Gospel Knowledge section). You know all that material. Giving these discussions is just like a home teaching or visiting teaching assignment.

The new-member discussions are imperative for the retention of converts. They help these new members understand more about the gospel now that they have been baptized.

## Fellowshipping

An important step in retaining new members is ensuring they make a social transition in the Church. They must make friends—find a support group—so that they want to change their lifestyles, to abandon habits and activities that are inappropriate. They must have access to the sociality of the Saints—the fellowshipping, the coming to church, and the going to meetings and activities so that people will be able to tell them how nice it is to see them. And when they start doing that, their lives will change because they feel like part of the kingdom. You might call it a community of the Saints. When you feel that sense of community, you want to be involved with it—with all that love and friendliness and common cause. This is why it's very important to take along a member or stake missionary, so new members can make the social connection to the gospel that will help keep them active.

The other day I was ready to teach my institute class and I looked at one girl whose close friend hadn't arrived yet. And I said, "Hi! How you doing today?"

"Oh good Brother Ed. I'm great." Her name was Alicia. She was sitting there and pretty soon her friend Angela walked in the door. Angela caught Alicia's eye; she came in and sat down. "Hi!" They smiled as they greeted one another, and they were just so happy together. They just thought it was so great to be together. And I thought, *They come to this class to learn, but they also come because of the sociality and love they feel.* Never, ever let a person feel unnoticed or unloved. When you go to your wards and you see the little children going to Primary, walk up and say, "Hi there, young man, you're going to be a great missionary." That's going to make him feel good. When you see those young girls, say, "Hi there! You'll look so good dressed in white when you're married in the temple." In other words, let everybody know that you care about them and give them hope and confidence. That's the sociality of the Saints—fellowshipping and loving because we truly, truly care.

As President Hinckley has taught us, everyone needs a friend, everyone needs a responsibility, and everyone needs to be nurtured by the good word of God ("Strengthening New Members," *Church News*, 29 Nov. 1997). And this is what we do as missionaries working in the local units. Always have a list of the new converts and make sure you visit them on a regular basis. It teaches us in Moroni 6:4 that converts' names were kept so that they could be nurtured by the good word of God.

### Emphasize Daily Prayer and Scripture Study

Another element of retention and activation is emphasizing the importance of personal prayer and daily scripture study. Although this principle was taught before your convert was baptized, we must emphasize that a testimony is something we must work to retain. Elder O. Leslie Stone stated:

> To obtain and retain a testimony of the gospel, a person must live the gospel; and to live it, he must know it; and to know it, he must study it. We cannot have a testimony of a subject about which we do not have some understanding or knowledge. When we have prepared ourselves, the Holy Ghost, who is also known as the Spirit of Truth, will manifest the truth of all things to us ("The Message: Testimony," *New Era,* July 1979, 4).

In your introduction to the missionary discussions booklet, you'll find the first thing discussed is teaching your investigators how to

pray and committing them to pray. This is not an incidental place-
ment; it is likely there because it is very important to begin doing, but
also to keep doing—even after baptism. This daily spiritual nourishing must develop into a lifelong habit.

The Lord said, "Verily, verily I say unto you, ye must watch and
pray always, lest ye be tempted." And then added, "For Satan desireth
to . . . sift you as wheat" (see 3 Ne. 18:15, 18). Even in our own individual lives, if we don't pray, and if we don't search the scriptures,
we'll be tempted and then we'll be less active in some part of the
gospel. We may attend our meetings, but we'll be less active in being
Saints of the Lord Jesus Christ. Personal prayer is absolutely imperative to being strong in the gospel.

Guess what else is absolutely imperative? Well, the second topic in
the missionary discussion booklet covers how to invite people to read,
study, and ponder the Book of Mormon. Everyone must be diligent
in searching the scriptures so temptation will not lead them astray.

Laman and Lemuel asked Nephi what the rod of iron in their
father's dream was all about. Nephi responded that "the [rod of iron] was
the word of God; and whoso would hearken unto [it] . . . they would
never perish; neither could the temptations and the fiery darts of the
adversary overpower them unto blindness, to lead them away to destruc-
tion" (1 Ne. 15:24). The only way you can get to the tree of life (eternal
life) is by holding to the rod. That's the word of the Lord. There is no
other way. And when temptations and trials come over us—the mists of
darkness—there's only one way through, and that is by holding to the
rod. We are counseled to live by every word that proceedeth forth from
the mouth of the Lord (see D&C 84:43–46), for the words of Christ
will tell us all things that we should do (see 2 Ne. 32:3).

Each individual soul—missionary, mother or father, new convert, or
the teenagers at home—must search the scriptures, and we must fast and
pray in order that we not be tempted beyond that which we can endure.
This is a vital truth we must be sure our new converts understand.

### Continually Visit

It's been said that people don't care how much you know until
they know how much you care. Do you really care about your new

converts? Do you really want them to stay active, or do you just want to baptize them so you can have five baptisms for the month? We baptize people so they can come unto Christ. Our duty as missionaries is to help them press forward with steadfastness; this is why we make continual visits. Remember, when we're making visits to the people, it is important that we live the principle in Doctrine and Covenants 108:7—to "strengthen [each other] . . . in all [our] doings." In other words, at every moment as we open our mouths—in our conversation, as we say our prayers, as we exhort our brothers and sisters to come back or stay strong, in all of our doings—we're doing everything we can to help people continually return to the Lord. Make sure you enter the names of new converts in the area control book. And visiting them with members is even better. Make sure you do all you can to help the fruit remain.

*Love, Love, Love*

Finally, love is a critical element in retaining new converts. People need to know that they're loved. People need to find joy within the Church and kingdom of God; otherwise it's very hard to be motivated.

Once, while I was a mission president, I met with an elders quorum president, and I said, "Hi there, how're you doing? Will you do this? Will you do that? Will you give me these names?"

And he thought, *Who is this wild man?* And he didn't like me.

And I thought, *Why don't you want to be a missionary? Everyone's supposed to be a missionary.* I became sad and upset. It was my third week as the mission president in England, and I was praying. I said, "Heavenly Father," and I began to cry. "This isn't fair. They're not doing their part. I'm working and no one wants to work, and this isn't right."

And then a voice came to me, and the voice said, "Ed my son, I didn't ask you to come here to judge them; I asked you to come here to love them." My heart was softened and my life changed in a moment. Love the members. Love the new converts. Love them so much that they will feel the Spirit that you feel. You love them so much that they'll want to love like you do; they'll feel like the sons of Mosiah. They won't be able to bear that any human soul should endure endless torment. You will know when charity is in your heart, as missionaries and members, because you'll want to share the gospel with your fellowmen.

Jesus told his disciples, "A new commandment I give unto you, That ye love one another; as I have loved you, that ye also love one another. By this shall all men know that ye are my disciples, if ye have love one to another" (John 13:34–35).

When people know you care, then they are willing to change. I would write the new English converts and ask them to tell me about their conversion. They would say, "The reason I was converted, President Pinegar, was because I felt the love of the missionaries so much that I had to listen to what they said. While listening I felt the Spirit and I knew I just had to be baptized." You see, love is important and must be felt. Friendshipping is one of the first steps toward showing our love.

The following account from Elder Robert D. Hales describes the power that the love of one senior couple can have on an entire branch.

> Missionary couples provide stability with their friendship-ping and leadership skills in areas where the Church is in its infancy. I learned this firsthand while serving as a mission president in England. I assigned a couple who had been serving in the visitors' center to working a small, struggling unit. They were somewhat fearful of having to leave the "save haven" of the visitors' center. But with faith they went to work. Within six months, a unit that had 15 to 20 people coming to sacrament meeting had over 100 attending because of this couple's fellow-shipping and working with the priesthood. To this day, they and their children refer to that time as the greatest experience of their lives.
>
> Another couple recently served in a small village south of Santiago, Chile. They had no Spanish skills and were apprehensive about being in a different country so far from the comforts of home. But they plunged in with total dedication, loving and serving the people. Before long, the small branch grew from 12 to 75 members. When it came time for them to leave, the entire branch rented a bus so they could go to the airport, four hours away, and say good-bye to their special friends (*Ensign*, May 2001, 25–26).

Remember what we're here for—to love people as Christ loved, and to bring people into the Church and keep them there. This is the greatest work on the earth, and if we can help the fruit remain, great will be our harvest of joy in this life and the life to come.

## Reclaiming the Less Active

We work with new converts and we also work with the less active—those who have strayed, people who have not made the best choices. I have found that in the Church and kingdom of God, whenever a person goes astray, they have been tempted to perhaps do something and have succumbed, or they simply didn't feel that the Church held anything for them personally. They were in a state where these things could happen; where pride, or greed, or lust, or selfishness, or jealousy, or apathy, or ignorance, or even the precepts of men, or the fear of men, or unbelief and vanity, or hypocrisy, or anger became part of their life, and they became less active. Another reason people become less active is because they feel a lack of love—no one cares. The psalmist wrote, "I looked on my right hand, and beheld, but there was no man that would know me: refuge failed me; no man cared for my soul" (Ps. 142:4). Feeling unloved is a major cause of inactivity in the Church.

There are four basic groups of less-actives: lifetime less-active members who often raise their families in inactivity; new converts who have fallen away, usually in their first year as members; active members who slip into transgression, or for some other reason fall away; and youth who fall away due to the philosophies of men and the influence of their peers.

### Gather Information and Pray for the Spirit

There are some things to remember in our visits to less-active people. Gather as much information as you can about the family before the visit. Visit with the bishop or their home teachers. Make sure you get only the information that's appropriate so you can better understand their needs. Let the home teacher know about your plan to visit. Remember that the missionaries are to visit the less active as part of our member work in missionary service. This is part of being a full-time minister for the Lord Jesus Christ.

Some valuable information to gather might be: (1) Are they a part-member family? (2) What is their marital status? (3) When were they baptized? (4) When was the last time they came to Church? (5) When was the last time they had home teachers? (6) What are their major concerns?

These kinds of things are valuable to know. Then, before your first visit, pray for the Spirit of the Lord to tell you all things you need to do before you go. Pray for sensitivity to what they might be going through, and for the ability to discern their needs and concerns. Remember, the Lord will prepare a way.

### Visiting with Less-Active Members

Your first visit should always be short and effective. Be sincere, and show love and concern for the people. Introduce yourselves, tell them you'd like to speak with them. Ask if this is a convenient time—if not, you'll return. Tell them a little about yourself. If they were converts, ask them about the missionaries who taught them. There's something that happens when that occurs. When converts recall the missionaries who taught them, they become very tender and sensitive to the Spirit.

For example, I remember that once I sent an elder to High Wycombe for his first area. He arrived in England and the missionaries were making less-active visits. He was taught these very things—to ask less-actives about the missionary who taught them. Well, Elder Kennard did, and the man answered, "Oh, she was a wonderful lady. Her name was Sister Loretta Johnson."

Well, Elder Kennard paled, and then he blurted out, "That's my mother. My mother taught you." They were so excited they could hardly stand it, to think that here he was called on a mission, his first area was High Wycombe, and he goes to make the less-active visits, and who does he visit? His mother's less-active convert. Needless to say, the fire was rekindled. Brother Eastley, the inactive member, came back to the Church. Not only that, but his wife, who was not a member, joined the Church as well. Those feelings converts have about their missionaries are always special in their hearts. The Lord knows that, and He certainly works in marvelous ways.

Be sure you express sincere interest in their feelings and their concerns, and discuss their real anxieties. You should be sweetly bold in order to get their concerns out in the open, but most of all, use love and tenderness so as to better understand their true concerns.

### Commit Them to Something

In every visit be sure you encourage them to make and keep at least one commitment. Whether it's just the commitment for a return visit, or a commitment to read the Book of Mormon, or a commitment to say their prayers, it is important that a return appointment be set up. As you continue to make these visits, make sure you remember that everyone is different and everyone is special. What might be best for one, may not be best for another.

### Correlation

And as you are visiting these less-actives, be sure you inform the ward council, and especially the ward mission leader. Then the ward can pool efforts to reactivate families. When you have a little boy who hasn't been baptized who's around that age, make sure you talk to the Primary president. Or if you have a beautiful young girl who's about fourteen years old, make sure the Young Women's presidency and the Mia Maid class can visit her. Make sure you correlate your work so everyone in the ward is involved to bless their lives. This is absolutely essential. Continued visits from everyone are important in helping them feel the Spirit and in helping them make and keep their commitments.

### Be Sensitive and Discern Their Concerns

We must always be careful not to hurt feelings, or give the wrong impression of who we are and what we care about—remember that we represent the Lord Jesus Christ and His Church. Never be defensive or argumentative, and don't worry about whether you're comfortable, but worry about whether you can help them feel more comfortable. Remember that you are there to repair broken bridges and take down walls, you are there to heal wounds and serve. If you feel nervous about this calling—afraid of what you might find or how welcome you'll be, you might do well to be calmed by some of the words of a famous prayer:

Lord, make me an instrument of Your peace.

Where there is hatred, let me sow love;

Where there is injury, let me sow pardon;

Where there is doubt, let me sow faith;

Where there is despair, let me sow hope;

Where there is darkness, let me sow light;

Where there is sadness, let me sow joy.


O, Divine Master,

Grant that I may not so much seek

To be consoled as to console;

To be understood as to understand;

To be loved as to love . . .

—Saint Francis of Assisi


We are simply there to be instruments of His peace, messengers of His gospel. If we go with a prayer in our hearts, and have lived worthy of the Spirit, the Lord will open doors that we thought were sealed shut.

When working with hesitant less-actives, and especially in trying to discern and resolve their concerns, consider the following:

1. *Their souls are precious:* You must put that belief into action so they know that you really care.

2. *Do you really know how they feel and what they are thinking?* Have you asked enough find-out questions? For example: "How did you feel when you attended church? How did you feel when you read the Book of Mormon? Will you come

with us to visit Sister so-and-so?" All of a sudden, some unrealized concerns may surface. But, you must understand, you'll never know their real condition until you've asked enough questions to know how they really feel and what they are really thinking.

3. *Have you used the Book of Mormon as a method of conversion?* Is there a passage or story in the Book of Mormon that can strengthen them?

4. *Have they felt the Spirit and, more importantly, are they aware of it?* You must help them identify it and recognize it in their lives.

5. *Have you gained a commitment?* Invite them to make a commitment when they feel the Spirit.

Now, after our less-active brothers and sisters have felt that Spirit, and they've been made aware of it, you help them resolve their concerns and make and keep their commitments. Make sure that you invite them properly, so that they'll have the power to keep the commitments that the Lord would have them keep.

We do this by using the "*Will you*" introduction. This requires a yes or no answer. Many times missionaries are afraid to do so because investigators could say "no." The blessing of the *"will you"* invitation is that if investigators have concerns, they will surface with the invitation to the commitment. This is vital, because people cannot progress when they have unresolved concerns. If they will not commit, you simply ask them if there is something about the commitment that makes them uncomfortable, or if they are concerned about something.

When you learn that concern, you can resolve it with a discussion—disclosing new information or reviewing a doctrine or principle, thereby calming their fears. You can also help them with simple encouragement, a special scripture, relating a personal experience, or by inspired words from the Holy Ghost (see D&C 100:5–6).

If they cannot commit to the particular thing you've invited them to do, then make it less difficult by asking them to do something less worrisome. For example, if you get "no" several times, you can simply decrease the difficulty of the request until you get a "yes." For instance, *"Will you* read four chapters in the Book of Mormon?"

"No."

"Then will you read a chapter?"

"No."

"Then will you read a few verses?" "Will you pray about reading?" "Will you let us come and talk to you about the Book of Mormon?" "Will you . . ."

"Ok."

See! The worst thing they can say is no. And that shouldn't stop you from leaving them with a commitment—no matter how small—because people can change no faster than they can make and keep commitments. And always arrange for a follow-up to help them.

## Conclusion

We must feel like Alma and the sons of Mosiah. As they were going to visit the Zoramites who had gone astray, Alma prayed, "Oh Lord, will thou grant unto us that we may have success in bringing them again unto thee in Christ. Behold, O Lord, their souls are precious, and many of them are our brethren; therefore, give unto us, O Lord, power and wisdom that we may bring these, our brethren, again unto thee" (Alma 31:34–35). The same prayer applies to whether we're bringing them for the first time, trying to keep them, or bringing them back to Christ.

Always remember that we should work just as hard to retain as we do to baptize. The joy of a strong, steadfast convert is a joy that transcends earthly honors. It is as if the person you help bring into the Church is literally a member of your personal family—for we are all the family of Christ. May we remember that our duty is not just to baptize, but to help the fruit of our labors remain; this way, we can all rejoice in each other again in that great celestial family reunion!

# CHAPTER 10

## STANDING FOR THE CAUSE OF CHRIST:

## CONSECRATION AND THE KINGDOM

Everyone seeks happiness. Everyone wants to feel good, experience joy, and be free from pain and discontent. And that's what our Heavenly Father wants for us as well. The Prophet Joseph Smith taught that the design of our existence is happiness (see *History of the Church* 5:134–135). True happiness is defined as a condition that has some lasting influence and value. The state of happiness is reserved for those who keep the commandments and endure to the end—then they will enter a state of never-ending happiness (see Mosiah 2:41).

Happiness is a state of being, *not* a state of ownership or worldly attainment. Don't let success and happiness depend on possessions or positions or comparisons of the things of the world—they will all eventually fade away. Happiness and joy is knowing that you have enriched the lives of others by bringing them unto Christ, which brings them lasting joy and peace. Enjoy the journey of life. Find joy in the simple things of life along the way. Senior missionaries have shared their happiness in doing missionary work and have often said, "It was the greatest time of our lives. I have never felt so good. I never realized how much good a couple could do. I want to serve missions until I die. This is the greatest joy I have ever felt since raising our children."

This greatest joy comes from standing for the cause of Christ. And from the beginning of time, this state of being has been described by the prophets of God as Zion. Enoch and his people found it. The Nephites found it for two hundred years after Christ's visit. This state of being is also a state of mind, or a state of the heart—of the pure in heart. It is Zion.

Zion is not only "the pure in heart," but it is a place, a people, and a state of world peace, prosperity, and joy. And we can take the steps to begin building it today.

## Creating a Zion Society Through Consecration

In his talk entitled, "Becoming a Zion Society: Six Principles," R. Quinn Gardner said:

> Consecration and sanctification of the *heart* is what creates Zion—*the pure in heart* (see D&C 29:34). Repeatedly in scripture, we see this same cleansing process occur in the lives of the Lord's faithful Saints. King Benjamin's people, moved upon by the purifying power of the Spirit, had their "*hearts . . . changed through faith on his name*" (Mosiah 5:7). Helaman tells us of a faithful group who grew "firmer and firmer in the faith of Christ . . . even to the purifying and the sanctification of their hearts, *which sanctification cometh because of their yielding their hearts unto God*" (Hel. 3:35; italics in the original) (*Ensign*, Feb. 1979, 31).

As we grow "firmer and firmer in the faith of Christ," we truly purify and sanctify our hearts, thereby becoming a Zion people. It is only then that we can change the outside world, bringing about the geographical and spiritual Zion prophesied of from the beginning of this earth.

The Lord has asserted that all we must do to build Zion is keep His commandments: "Behold, I say unto you, keep my commandments, and seek to bring forth and establish the cause of Zion" (D&C 6:6). In general conference Elder Robert D. Hales echoes what the Lord has said—that Zion comes a step at a time by keeping our temple covenants, by living the higher law of consecration. He asserts that serving missions is a fulfillment of that law.

> There are two unique times in our lives when we can truly live the law of consecration and devote ourselves in full-time service to

the Lord. One is as a young man or woman serving a full-time mission. The other is the unique time you are given after having fulfilled the requirements of earning a living. The latter could be called the "patriarchal years," when you can draw upon the rich experiences of a lifetime, go out as a couple, and consecrate yourselves fully as servants of the Lord (*Ensign,* May 2001, 27).

This is indeed a "unique time" to consecrate our service to the Lord. It is a chance to learn firsthand what Moses described when he told of the Lord's proclamation that a Zion people are "of one heart and one mind, and [who] dwel[l] in righteousness; [and who have] no poor among them" (Moses 7:18). Laboring as missionaries among the Lord's children, we truly become "of one heart, and one mind," and not only do we work to relieve temporal poverty through humanitarian work, but we relieve spiritual "poverty" as well. These day-to-day labors do indeed bring forth Zion. The following story from one senior couple exemplifies this truth perfectly.

> While serving as country directors in humanitarian work in the Philippines, we were asked by a stake president who taught history in the high school in Gapan, Philippines, if we would fund the putting of a roof over two classrooms that had none. He said if we could, the school superintendent would allow him to teach seminary in the room as much as he needed.
>
> After making our request, however, [the committee decided] not to approve it. It was heartbreaking to the stake president. Feeling his hurt, we asked that the committee [still] approve our request of donating text books, computers, and some machines which were part of our original request. It was approved. [After that they changed their minds about the roof as well.]
>
> Prior to this time, the stake president was teaching 100 seminary students in the stake center, of which 10 were nonmembers. This was early morning seminary. After . . . the approval of books and other items, word got out and the stake president said to us, "Guess how many seminary students we have?"
>
> I said, "I don't know."

President Salvador said, "Three hundred—and two hundred of those are nonmembers." What a joy to see what a humanitarian gift meant to those people.

The national average of books per student was one book per thirteen students. Our donation through our Church was 14,000 books. It made a significant impact on the school. The principal was so grateful that she talked the mayor into donating funds to renovate the library with new shelves and air conditioning.

We were invited to the open house of the completed library. President Salvador again said, "Guess how many seminary students we have?" We said we had no idea. He said, "Four hundred, and three hundred are nonmembers." He also told us that because of the renovating of the library and the mayor getting funds from local businessmen, that the professional people of the city were starting to take missionary lessons.

The stake president had been concerned about the roof of the school, and the total community was affected by the results.

One of the teachers told us she was taking missionary lessons because of our church's involvement in her school. She told us she had discussed this with her minister, who told her to not do that, for we were not Christians. She told him if there was any church who did Christian things it was our church—and that her church could learn from us on loving [and] Christian principles.

This was one of about seventy-two projects we were involved in during our humanitarian mission in the Philippines. We would have missed out on one of the greatest experiences of our life had we not gone on our first mission.

—Elder LaMont and Sister Lula Marie Henriksen


## Sacrificing for the Cause of Christ

The joy and fulfillment that comes from sacrificing for the Lord goes on forever. Why? Because we ultimately become like that which we love. Harold B. Lee reminded us of this principle:

> Someone [once] said, "If you live long enough in the presence of an ideal you will grow to be like him." President [David O.] McKay lifted this ideal to a high standard when he said, "We become what we love. Joseph Smith loved the Savior and became like him" (*The Teachings of Harold B. Lee*, 617).

Just as Joseph Smith, and all the other prophets that have become like the Savior, we too will become like the person we serve; if that is our Savior, we'll become like Him—full of charity, full of love, and able to enter into a state of never-ending happiness. Surely we understand that only in living and sharing the gospel of Jesus Christ do we become truly happy.

Living the gospel—truly living it—requires sacrifice. The Savior was the ultimate example of sacrifice. And he asked us to do the same. Senior couples across the globe are heeding that call—sacrificing sometimes their very lives. One of my dear friends, who was a great player for BYU basketball, lived a life of service and sacrifice. His story of missionary service is described in the *Church News*.

> Three years ago, Elder Joseph Richey had just been admitted to a Fresno, Calif., hospital where he was told by his doctor that he was dying of leukemia. He was told that 85 percent of the people with this condition died within a very short time. "I've never considered myself part of the 85 percent," Elder Richey said. "I'm in the top 15 percent. Tell me what happens to them."
>
> The doctor replied, "Some live for three, even five years and some longer."
>
> "That's what I'll do," he said.
>
> Joe Richey, a paving contractor who had been operating his paving equipment up to the day he was hospitalized, had reason to believe he really was in the top 15 percent. He attended BYU in the 1950s where he played basketball and was selected for All-American honors. He was a member of the 1951 BYU team that won the National Invitational Tournament championship.
>
> The visit with the doctor began what was the hardest 40 days of Elder Richey's life. He was treated first with

chemotherapy and then fought the resulting yeast infections with equally strong and painful medications. "When the pain and misery became unbearable," Elder Richey said, "I remember telling my Father in Heaven that I was ready to go if that is what He wanted, but I really wanted to stay."

Elder Richey proved he was indeed among the top 15 percent. He recovered, and a year later, he and his wife, Sharon, were called to the England Birmingham Mission as proselyting and leadership missionaries. They were instrumental in the establishment of the March Branch and had one baptism before Elder Richey again became seriously ill and returned to Fresno for treatment.

Three months later, after fighting his way back, he and his wife again returned to the mission field—but not before they had committed a Fresno family of five to baptism. Within two weeks of returning to the mission, they baptized a mother and a 16-year-old daughter. Elder Richey, however, had been seriously weakened by his recent illness. This ultimately caused a return of his leukemia. He continued to serve right up until 12 days before his death on April 4, 1995.

Elder Richey truly was in the top 15 percent. He and his wife were part of an elect group of 1,800 senior missionary couples who serve throughout the world. They do it because they love the Lord and want to bring the happiness of the gospel into the lives of others ("Missionary Moments: Top 15 Percent," *Church News,* 27 May 1995).

Elder Richey's story exemplifies the ultimate sacrifice, and is a modern example of the scripture in John which states: "Greater love hath no man than this, that a man lay down his life for his friends" (15:13). This is the gospel of Christ: love unto salvation. As we perform missionary work—simply being out there—aren't we in essence a living proclamation of the gospel of Christ? The giving of our time and talents, and putting aside our fears, pains, and weaknesses—exchanging them for faith—is also a great sacrifice, and, as illustrated in the following article in the *Church News,* the Lord is aware of that sacrifice. The resulting blessings in Zion, and in our personal lives, are truly remarkable.

Missionary couples in the Monterrey area are proving to be "saviours on Mount Zion," preparing for the day when there will be many fewer less-active members in Mexico, according to the Mexico North Area presidency.

These senior missionaries, half of whom did not speak Spanish before arriving, are making significant contributions in such areas as reactivations, leadership training, conversions, music training, membership records, family history work, missionary health, and even in local medicine.

"These couples are literally transforming lives, wards, and stakes," said Elder John M. Madsen of the Seventy and a counselor in the Mexico North Area presidency. "They bring a strength and spirit with them that is priceless and invaluable. We've seen wonderful progress. . . ."

[President Garry R. Flake of the Mexico South Mission' observed that if the missions had enough couples so that one could be assigned to each ward for a few months each year, "great things would happen."

The love the couples have for each other shines as an example to young missionaries, an estimated one-third of whom are converts of less than four years and who are typically the only members of their families in the Church, said Pres. Flake.

And, he said, because of the extended family system that thrives in the culture, older people are highly respected in Mexico. "The Spirit emanates from couples. . . and it opens doors and opens hearts. . . ."

A former missionary to Mexico, Sister [Gladys] Powell was called to serve in the area presidency office. In the evenings, [she and her husband] serve in many additional ways, including visiting less-active members and teaching piano and hymn-conducting lessons to 20–30 pupils who are from ages 8–50.

"After five months of teaching lessons, we realized that these students needed to learn to play the hymns, not in four or five years, but right now," she said. She obtained simplified hymns and soon their students were playing in sacrament meetings. One 14-year-old named Jorge has been a particularly adept student.

A member commented to them: "You can't imagine the difference music has made in our ward. Last Sunday, we had 30 people bear their testimonies. We've never had that many before. I know it is because of the music Jorge has been playing."

Elder Powell, who doesn't speak Spanish, said: "The people here are so patient you can feel their love."

"It is better to serve rather than just say you can't do it because you can't speak the language—the language is love."

Elder Marion and Sister Bonnie Peterson of Mesa (Ariz.) 42nd ward began serving in March of 1993.

Neither of the Petersons spoke Spanish when they received their mission call. In addition, Sister Peterson's back ailment was so painful that she couldn't sit through a meeting. She had to stand through half her classes at the Missionary Training Center. When it came time to travel to Mexico, she did so in the back of their truck, lying down.

However, since their arrival in Mexico they have touched lives from the elite medical community to children they've met on the streets. And sister Peterson's back has improved so that she can "sit through five hours of meetings."

They began by asking members to write their names on a pad. The Petersons then took the pad home and memorized the names. Local members accompanied them as they visited many less-active families, audited hundreds of membership records, and trained priesthood leaders. And, for the first time in her life, Sister Peterson taught piano lessons.

Elder Peterson, an orthopedic surgeon, spends his service hours instructing doctors at the university hospital in Monterrey.

"They call me 'Dr. Elder,'" he said. He also trains missionaries and mission presidents in ways to maintain health.

As they walk along the streets, they meet many children. Elder Peterson entertains them with a magic trick—the only one he knows. Over the months, they have met with groups of children often, teaching them stories from the Book of Mormon and how to sing the Church Hymns.

"There are a lot of grand people we have found," said Elder Peterson. Elder Carl J. and Sister Rita Beecroft of the Ventura (Calif.) 3rd Ward began serving in November of 1993. Elder Beecroft, a former stake president, suffered health problems that they felt would prevent their serving a mission.

"He felt like we couldn't serve because of a disability he has with his speaking, and his walking," she said. "But we decided that we could serve on a mission as well as we could serve anywhere else."

Since their arrival, "the Spanish language has come to him more fluently," she said. "His walking ability has not been a problem."

The Beecrofts have completed a mountain of family history work that includes training 51 stake presidents, instructing local members to input their family history on computers, clearing names for the temple, setting up several new family history centers, and training ward and stake family history specialists.

"We feel very blessed to be here and are most grateful for the experiences we've had," said Sister Beecroft.

"As our mission winds down, we are saddened to think of leaving the good Saints of Mexico."

She said interest in family history work is increasing rapidly among the members of the Monterrey area.

"It is like a ripple effect—it increases more as more information gets to other Saints. Members in lots of stakes go to the Mexico City Temple on excursions and most of the members want to do the work themselves for their ancestors. . . ." ("Couples Bless Lives in Mexico," *Church News,* 26 March 1994).

## Conclusion

I know you understand the vision of the work, and that you are starting to understand the vision of your responsibility in building up the kingdom of God. When you were baptized you covenanted to be willing "to stand as witnesses of God at all times and in all things, and in all places" (Mosiah 18:9). To stand as a witness for God *always*. The young women of the Church know that as part of their theme, which they say every week. What do witnesses do? We testify. What do we testify of? That God is our Father, Jesus is the Christ, the Book of Mormon is true, Joseph Smith is a prophet, the gospel has been restored, the true Church is on the earth today, and we are led by a living prophet. We are witnesses. We testify. That's our duty and our joy.

"For they [you and me in the last days] were set to be a light unto the world" (D&C 103:9). The light of the world is the Lord Jesus Christ. The light that we possess is the amount of light of the Lord Jesus Christ we have within us. So we are sent to be a light unto the world. But that's only part of it. The rest of the verse reads, "And to be the saviors of men; And inasmuch as they are not the saviors of men" (in other words, if we're not out there with our light, helping people come unto Christ), "they [you and I] are as salt that has lost its savor" (v. 10), or in other words, become impure or have no value.

If we, as the salt of the earth, don't hold up our light, we've lost our savor, "and [are] thenceforth good for nothing but to be cast out and trodden under foot of men" (v. 10). This life is serious business—it's a testing and training ground for gods and goddesses. Think about that. We have been given much, and our business on this earth is to help Heavenly Father build His kingdom by blessing our brothers and sisters, and that's it. That's what we're here for.

But we are never alone in this calling, and we are also truly "unprofitable servants" (see Mosiah 2:21); for no matter what we do for the Lord, He gives us back more blessings than we know what to do with. We need not fear this calling.

I teach the senior missionaries every Wednesday at the MTC. I get to visit with them and often they express their feelings. They tell me of taking their fears and weaknesses before the Lord. They would ask for Him to bless them with things like courage, strength, and power to overcome their fears of whether or not a mission was right for them. The answer for so many is a resounding "Yes!" Then they come. They are happy, and they feel so good that they talk of extending their missions before they even leave the MTC!

One particular senior missionary expressed his reasons for being on a mission, in spite of his weaknesses and fears.

> This comes hard for me. I am not a literate man. I'm a mechanic. You want me to put down my feelings about why I'm here and how I feel about being here. I am here for several reasons:
>
> 1) The Lord through His prophets has told us this is where we should be.
>
> 2) I am a selfish man. I want the blessings I receive from doing the Lord's work. [Author's note: He's not selfish. He just likes to be happy and feel the joy of serving.]
>
> 3) On our other missions we met so many wonderful people that will always be our friends.
>
> 4) For the strength it gives our family because we have served. So far all of our grandsons and one granddaughter have served missions; and the rest are all planning to as they come of age.
>
> 5) We have worked hard on our first two missions, but we also had a great time. (My wife is talking about extending our 18-month mission, and we are still in the MTC.)
>
> 6) I LOVE IT!
>
> —One Happy Senior Missionary, MTC, 2001

We must gird up our loins and put our concerns behind us. We are chosen in the last days to bless our brothers and sisters—the children of God the Father. This is our responsibility, our joy, our glory, and the source of our happiness. May we all seek to serve as true disciples of Jesus Christ is my personal prayer. We can make a difference in the eternal lives of so many people. Now is the time, and we are the ones to take the gospel to every nation, kindred, tongue, and people. The field is white, are we ready to harvest?

# BIBLIOGRAPHY

Benson, Ezra Taft. *Come Listen to a Prophet's Voice.* Salt Lake City: Deseret Book Co., 1990.

Black, Don J. *A Pocket Full of Miracles: A Collection of Heartwarming True Stories.* Salt Lake City: Covenant Recordings, 1989.

Condie, Spencer J. *In Perfect Balance.* Salt Lake City: Bookcraft, 1993.

Franklin, Benjamin. *Poor Richard's Almanach.* New York: David McKay Company, Inc., 1976.

Grant, Heber J. *Gospel Standards: Selections from the Sermons and Writings of Heber J. Grant.* compiled by G. Homer Durham. Salt Lake City: *Improvement Era*, 1981.

Haight, David B. *A Light unto the World.* Salt Lake City: Deseret Book Co., 1997.

Hinkley, Gordon B. *Without Sacrifice There Is No True Worship.* Brigham Young University Speeches of the Year. Provo, Utah: BYU University Press, 1962.

Lee, Harold B. *The Teachings of Harold B. Lee.* edited by Clyde J. Williams. Salt Lake City: Bookcraft, 1996.

Maxwell, Neal A. *If Thou Endure It Well.* Salt Lake City: Bookcraft, 1996.

Monson, Thomas. *Live the Good Life.* Salt Lake City: Deseret Book Co., 1998.

Pratt, Parely P. *Key to the Science of Theology.* Salt Lake City: Deseret Book Co., 1979.

Richards, LeGrand. *The Things That Matter.* Brigham Young University Speeches of the Year. Provo, Utah: BYU University Press, 1961.

Schweitzer, Albert. As quoted in *Especially for Mormons, Vol. 3.* Compiled by Stan and Sharon Miller. Provo, Utah: Kellirae Arts, 1990.

Smith, Joseph, Jr. *History of the Church.* Salt Lake City: Deseret Book Co., 1950.

Snow, Lorenzo. *The Teachings of Lorenzo Snow.* edited by Clyde J. Williams. Salt Lake City: Bookcraft, 1984.

Mother Teresa. *No Greater Love.* Novato, California: New World Library, 1997.

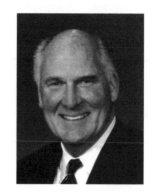

# ABOUT THE AUTHOR

Ed J. Pinegar graduated from Brigham Young University in 1956 with a degree in chemistry and mathematics. He attended dental school at the University of Southern California, during which time he taught early morning seminary.

Upon returning to Provo to begin his dental practice, he again taught early morning seminary and Book of Mormon and Gospel Principles and Practices classes at BYU. Brother Pinegar presently serves part time on the faculty at the Orem Institute of Religion at Utah Valley State College in Orem, Utah, and is a teacher at the Senior MTC in Provo.

Some of Brother Pinegar's former Church callings include: President of the England, London South Mission; President of the Missionary Training Center in Provo, Utah; and member of the Missionary Programs Advisory Committee.

Brother Pinegar has produced numerous talk tapes, including several volumes of *Especially for Missionaries*. He has taught many Continuing Education programs and was a recipient of the Excellence in Teaching Award in 1979.

Brother Pinegar is married to Patricia Peterson Pinegar, who formerly served as General President of the Primary for the Church, and they are the parents of eight children, thirty grandchildren, and one great-grandchild.